A BALANCED MATHEMATICS PROGRAM INTEGRATING SCIENCE AND LANGUAGE ARTS

Unit Resource Guide
Unit 10
Using Decimals

THIRD EDITION

 KENDALL/HUNT PUBLISHING COMPANY
4050 Westmark Drive   Dubuque, Iowa 52002

A TIMS® Curriculum
University of Illinois at Chicago

UIC The University of Illinois at Chicago

The original edition was based on work supported by the National Science Foundation under grant No. MDR 9050226 and the University of Illinois at Chicago. Any opinions, findings, and conclusions or recommendations expressed in this publication are those of the author(s) and do not necessarily reflect the views of the granting agencies.

Letter Home

Using Decimals

Date: _____

Dear Family Member:

In this unit the class will work with measurement to give students a better understanding of the meaning of decimals. We will use decimals by measuring length in meters, decimeters, centimeters, and millimeters. These measurement units are illustrated in the picture below. Linking our study of decimals with measurements will help your child visualize the relative size of decimal numbers. We will conduct an experiment, *Downhill Racer,* in which students roll toy cars or skates down ramps and measure how far the cars roll as we raise the ramp to different heights. For this experiment, have your child bring a toy car, roller skate, or other "rolling toy" to school. Toys that roll straight and far work best. Please label your child's toy with his or her name so there is no confusion when returning the toy.

Meters, decimeters, centimeters, and millimeters

You can help your child by providing additional mathematics opportunities at home. For example:

- Help your child measure objects around the house in meters, decimeters, and centimeters.
- Talk about decimals in everyday life. Car odometers, labels on packages, and statistics in newspapers offer opportunities to discuss the meaning of decimals.
- Practice the division facts for the twos and threes with your child. Your child will bring home *Triangle Flash Cards* to study these facts.

Thank you for taking time to talk with your child about what he or she is doing in math. Please feel free to contact me with any questions, concerns, or comments about this unit.

Sincerely,

_____

Carta al hogar

Usando decimales

Fecha: _____

Estimado miembro de familia:

En esta unidad, la clase trabajará con las medición para dar a los estudiantes una mejor comprensión del significado de los decimales. Usaremos decimales al hacer mediciones en metros, decímetros, centímetros y milímetros. Estas unidades de medición se ilustran en el siguiente dibujo. La conexión del estudio de los decimales con las mediciones ayudará a su hijo/a a visualizar el tamaño relativo de los números decimales. Haremos un experimento llamado *Carrera cuesta abajo* en el que los estudiantes hacen rodar carritos o patines por rampas y miden hasta dónde ruedan los carritos a medida que levantamos la rampa a distintas alturas. Para este experimento, su hijo/a debe traer a la escuela un carrito de juguete, un patín u otro "juguete que ruede". Los mejores juguetes para este experimento son los que ruedan en línea recta y lejos. Por favor, coloque el nombre de su hijo/a en el juguete para que no haya confusiones cuando devolvamos los juguetes.

Metros, decímetros, centímetros y milímetros

Usted puede ayudar a su hijo/a dándole oportunidades matemáticas adicionales en casa. Por ejemplo:

- Ayude a su hijo/a a medir objetos de la casa en metros, decímetros y centímetros.
- Hablen acerca de los decimales en la vida cotidiana. Los cuentakilómetros/cuentamillas de los automóviles, las etiquetas de los paquetes y las estadísticas de los periódicos son buenas oportunidades para hablar sobre el significado de los decimales.
- Practique las tablas de división del dos y del tres con su hijo/a. Su hijo/a traerá estas tarjetas a casa para estudiar estas divisiones.

Gracias por tomarse el tiempo para hablar con su hijo/a acerca de lo que está haciendo en la clase de matemáticas. Por favor, comuníquese conmigo si tiene preguntas, inquietudes o comentarios sobre esta unidad.

Atentamente,

Table of Contents

Unit 10
Using Decimals

Unit 10

Outline
Using Decimals

Unit Summary

Estimated Class Sessions
12-14

The goal of this unit is for students to develop connections between decimals and physical models, pictures, real situations, symbols, and words. Students explore decimals as they measure lengths in meters, decimeters, centimeters, and millimeters. They learn to read, write, and order decimals to the hundredths. They make connections between common fractions and decimals.

Students use the TIMS Laboratory Method to complete the *Downhill Racer* lab. This unit also includes a game that practices comparing decimals. The Adventure Book, *Alberto in TenthsLand,* tells the story of a child who falls asleep in a library and dreams of a world where everything involves tenths. The DPP for this unit provides practice with and assesses the division facts for the twos and threes.

Major Concept Focus

- TIMS Laboratory Method
- *Adventure Book:* decimals
- best-fit lines
- fractional units of measure
- tenths and hundredths
- length in mm, dm, cm, and m
- common fractions
- reading, comparing, and writing decimals
- point graphs
- number sense for decimals
- Student Rubric: *Knowing*
- interpolation and extrapolation
- division facts for the twos and threes

Pacing Suggestions

This unit will take 12 to 14 days to complete depending on your students' familiarity with decimals. Students began their formal study of decimals in Grade 3 Unit 15.

- Lesson 4 *Downhill Racer* provides connections to science. Students can collect the data for the lab during science time.
- Lesson 5 *Decimal Hex* is an optional lesson. It is a challenging game that provides practice comparing decimals.
- Lesson 6 *Alberto in TenthsLand* is an *Adventure Book* story that provides a connection to language arts. It is based on *The Adventures of Alice in Wonderland.* Alberto grows ten times larger than normal and shrinks to one-tenth his normal size. Students can read the story as part of language arts time.

Assessment Indicators

Use the following Assessment Indicators and the *Observational Assessment Record* that follows the Background section in this unit to assess students on key ideas.

A1. Can students represent decimals using number lines (metersticks) and base-ten pieces?

A2. Can students read and write decimals to hundredths?

A3. Can students skip count by tenths and hundredths?

A4. Can students measure length to the nearest mm, cm, dm, and m?

A5. Can students collect, organize, graph, and analyze data?

A6. Do students demonstrate fluency with the division facts for the 2s and 3s?

Unit Planner

	Lesson Information	Supplies	Copies/Transparencies
Lesson 1 **m, dm, cm, mm** URG Pages 30–45 SG Pages 270–275 DAB Pages 163–166 DPP A–D HP Parts 1–2 *Estimated Class Sessions* **2**	**Activity** Students measure objects in the classroom first to the nearest whole meter, and then to the nearest tenth, hundredth, and thousandth of a meter. They discuss appropriate units of measure for various situations. **Math Facts** DPP items B and C provide practice with division facts. Task D provides practice with base-ten shorthand and multiplying with multiples of 10. **Homework** 1. Assign *Questions 1–2* in the Homework section of the *m, dm, cm, mm* Activity Pages after Part 1. 2. Assign *Question 3* in the Homework section of the *m, dm, cm, mm* Activity Pages after Part 3. 3. Assign Parts 1 and 2 of the Home Practice. **Assessment** 1. Use the *Observational Assessment Record* to document students' abilities to measure length to the nearest mm, cm, dm, and m. 2. Set up a performance assessment task in which students measure specified objects.	• 1 or 2 metersticks per student group • about 10 skinnies and 10 bits per student group • 1 meter of string per student • 1 centimeter ruler per student • masking tape • 1 envelope for storing flash cards per student	• 1 transparency of *Class Measurement Tables* DAB Page 163 • 1 copy of *Observational Assessment Record* URG Pages 13–14 to be used throughout this unit
Lesson 2 **Tenths** URG Pages 46–61 SG Pages 276–282 DAB Pages 167–171 DPP E–H HP Parts 4–5 *Estimated Class Sessions* **2-3**	**Activity** Students work with decimal notation for tenths. The emphasis is on connections between base-ten pieces, shorthand, and written notation for common and decimal fractions. **Math Facts** DPP item G provides practice with division facts. **Homework** 1. Complete the *Exploring Tenths* Activity Pages in the *Discovery Assignment Book* as homework. 2. Assign Parts 4 and 5 of the Home Practice. **Assessment** Use the *Observational Assessment Record* to document students' abilities to translate between concrete, pictorial, and symbolic representations of decimals.	• 2 packs, 14 flats, and 30 skinnies per student pair • 1 meterstick per student pair • overhead base-ten pieces	• 1 transparency of *Tenths Helper* DAB Page 167

	Lesson Information	Supplies	Copies/Transparencies

Lesson 3

Hundredths

URG Pages 62–79
SG Pages 283–287
DAB Pages 173–177

DPP I–N
HP Part 3

Estimated Class Sessions
3

Activity
Students work with decimal notation for hundredths. The emphasis is on connections between base-ten pieces, shorthand, and written notation for common and decimal fractions.

Math Facts
DPP Bits K and M provide math facts practice.

Homework
1. Assign the *More Hundredths* Activity Pages in the *Discovery Assignment Book* after Part 1.
2. Assign the Homework section, *Playing Hundredths, Hundredths, Hundredths,* in the *Student Guide* after Part 2.
3. Assign Home Practice Part 3.

Assessment
1. Score the *Linda's Base-Ten Pieces* Assessment Blackline Master using the Knowing dimension of the *TIMS Multidimensional Rubric.*
2. Use the *Observational Assessment Record* to document students' abilities to translate between different representations of decimals.

• 2 packs, 14 flats, 30 skinnies, and 50 bits per student pair
• overhead base-ten pieces, optional

• 1 copy of *Linda's Base-Ten Pieces* URG Page 73 per student
• 1 transparency of *Shorthand and Fractions Table* DAB Page 177
• 1 copy of *TIMS Multidimensional Rubric* TIG, Assessment section, optional
• 1 transparency or poster of Student Rubric: *Knowing* TIG, Assessment section

Lesson 4

Downhill Racer

URG Pages 80–103
SG Pages 288–295

DPP O–V

Estimated Class Sessions
4

Lab
Students collect, organize, graph, and analyze data as they study the relationship between the height of a ramp and the distance a car rolls. They use decimals to measure the distance the car rolls.

Math Facts
DPP Bit Q provides practice with division facts.

Homework
1. Assign some or all of the questions in the Explore section.
2. Assign the Homework section on the *Downhill Racer* Lab Pages after students complete the *Roberto's Data* Assessment Blackline Master.

Assessment
1. Use *Roberto's Data* Assessment Blackline Master to assess students' understanding of the *Downhill Racer* lab.
2. Use the *Observational Assessment Record* to document students' abilities to collect, organize, graph, and analyze data.
3. Transfer information from the Unit 10 *Observational Assessment Record* to students' *Individual Assessment Record Sheets.*

• 1 wood or metal ramp at least 50 cm long per student group
• 1 toy car or roller skate per student group
• 2–3 metersticks per student group
• 4–5 blocks or books of equal size per student group
• masking tape
• 1 calculator per student group

• 1 copy of *Roberto's Data* URG Pages 95–96 per student
• at least 3 copies of *Centimeter Graph Paper* URG Page 97 per student
• 1 copy of *Three-trial Data Table* URG Page 98 per student
• 1 transparency of *Centimeter Graph Paper* URG Page 97
• 1 copy of *Individual Assessment Record Sheet* TIG Assessment section per student, previously copied for use throughout the year

(Continued)

	Lesson Information	Supplies	Copies/ Transparencies
Lesson 5 **Decimal Hex** URG Pages 104–107 DAB Pages 179–181 *Estimated Class Sessions* **1**	OPTIONAL LESSON **Optional Game** As part of a game, students compare decimals. **Homework** Students take home the *Decimal Hex* Game Pages to play with family members. **Assessment** Use the *Observational Assessment Record* to note students' abilities to compare and order decimals.	• 2 same-color centimeter cubes as game markers per student • 1 clear plastic spinner or paper clip and pencil per student • base-ten pieces	
Lesson 6 **Alberto in TenthsLand** URG Pages 108–116 AB Pages 45–56 DPP W–X HP Part 6 *Estimated Class Sessions* **1**	**Adventure Book** The hero of this story falls asleep in the library and has a dream about a place called TenthsLand. He has a series of adventures in which he meets several fantastic creatures. Decimals and 10 percent are emphasized. **Math Facts** DPP item W is a quiz on the division facts for the twos and threes. Task X asks students to solve a division problem, write a story about it, and draw a picture. **Homework** 1. Have students read and discuss the *Adventure Book* with family members. 2. Assign Part 6 of the Home Practice. **Assessment** Use DPP Bit W to assess students on the division facts for the twos and threes.	• 1 calculator per student	

Preparing for Upcoming Lessons

Ask students to bring in toy cars, roller skates, or other things with wheels for the experiment in Lesson 4.

Connections

A current list of literature and software connections is available at *www.mathtrailblazers.com.* You can also find information on connections in the *Teacher Implementation Guide* Literature List and Software List sections.

Literature Connections

Suggested Titles

- Allen, Pamela. *Mr. Archimedes Bath.* HarperCollins Publishers, New York, 1998.
- Carroll, Lewis. *The Annotated Alice: The Definitive Edition. Alice's Adventures in Wonderland;* and *Through the Looking-Glass and What Alice Found There.* Introduction by Martin Gardner. Illustrated by John Tenniel. W.W. Norton, New York, 1999. (Lesson 6)
- Coffland, Jack and David. *Football Math: Touchdown Activities and Projects for Grades 4–8.* Good Year Books, Tucson, AZ, 1995.
- Gifford, Scott and Shmuel Thaler. *Piece =Part = Portion.* Tricycle Press, Berkeley, CA, 2003.
- Leedy, Loreen. *Fraction Action.* Holiday House, New York, 1996.
- LoPresti, Angeline Sparagna. *A Place for Zero.* Charlesbridge Publishing, Watertown, MA, 2003.
- Myller, Rolf. *How Big Is a Foot?* Yearling, New York, 1991.
- Owen, Claire. *A Simple System.* ETA/Cuisenaire, Vernon Hills, IL, 2005.
- Schwartz, David M. *Millions to Measure.* Harper Trophy, New York, 2006.

Software Connections

- *Fraction Attraction* develops understanding of fractions using fraction bars, pie charts, hundreds blocks, and other materials.
- *Graph Master* allows students to collect data and create their own graphs.
- *Ice Cream Truck* develops problem solving, money skills, and arithmetic operations.
- *Kid Pix* allows students to create their own illustrations.
- *Math Arena* is a collection of math activities that reinforces many math concepts.
- *Math Munchers Deluxe* provides practice in basic facts and finding equivalent fractions, decimals, and percents in an arcade-like game.
- *Math Mysteries: Fractions* develops problem solving with fractions.
- *Math Mysteries: Measurement* develops multistep problem solving with distance, weight, and capacity.
- *Math Workshop Deluxe* allows students to explore fractions and decimals.
- *Mighty Math Number Heroes* poses short-answer questions about fractions and number operations.
- *Tenth Planet: Fraction Operations* develops conceptual understanding of fraction operations.
- *TinkerPlots* allows students to record, compare, and analyze data in tables and graphs.

Teaching All Math Trailblazers Students

Math Trailblazers® lessons are designed for students with a wide range of abilities. The lessons are flexible and do not require significant adaptation for diverse learning styles or academic levels. However, when needed, lessons can be tailored to allow students to engage their abilities to the greatest extent possible while building knowledge and skills.

To assist you in meeting the needs of all students in your classroom, this section contains information about some of the features in the curriculum that allow all students access to mathematics. For additional information, see the Teaching the *Math Trailblazers* Student: Meeting Individual Needs section in the *Teacher Implementation Guide*.

Differentiation Opportunities in this Unit

Games

Use games to promote or extend understanding of math concepts and to practice skills with children who need more practice.

- *Hundredths, Hundredths, Hundredths* from Lesson 3 *Hundredths*
- Lesson 5 *Decimal Hex*

Laboratory Experiments

Laboratory experiments enable students to solve problems using a variety of representations including pictures, tables, graphs, and symbols. Teachers can assign or adapt parts of the analysis according to the student's ability. The following lesson is a lab:

- Lesson 4 *Downhill Racer*

Journal Prompts

Journal prompts provide opportunities for students to explain and reflect on mathematical problems. They can help both students who need practice explaining their ideas and students who benefit from answering higher order questions. Students with various learning styles can express themselves using pictures, words, and sentences. Teachers can alter journal prompts to suit students' ability levels. The following lessons contain a journal prompt:

- Lesson 1 *m, dm, cm, mm*
- Lesson 2 *Tenths*
- Lesson 3 *Hundredths*
- Lesson 4 *Downhill Racer*

DPP Challenges

DPP Challenges are items from the Daily Practice and Problems that usually take more than fifteen minutes to complete. These problems are more thought-provoking and can be used to stretch students' problem-solving skills. The following lesson has a DPP Challenge in it:

- DPP Challenge N from Lesson 3 *Hundredths*

Extensions

Use extensions to enrich lessons. Many extensions provide opportunities to further involve or challenge students of all abilities. Take a moment to review the extensions prior to beginning this unit. Some extensions may require additional preparation and planning. The following lesson contains an extension:

- Lesson 1 *m, dm, cm, mm*

Background
Using Decimals

In this unit students continue to develop their conceptual understanding of decimals. They engage in a series of activities in which they learn to make connections between different models of decimals: physical models, pictures, real situations, symbols, words, and common fractions. See Figure 1. Translating among these modes of representation—drawing a picture to go with a display of manipulatives or reading "4.3" aloud as "four and three-tenths"—helps students develop a strong grasp of the meaning of a decimal. This enables them to maneuver between the many contexts in which decimals appear. Research indicates that students with a solid conceptual understanding learn procedures for working with decimals more easily and can apply those procedures to problem situations more effectively (Ball, 1993; Behr & Post, 1992; Hiebert, Wearne & Taber, 1991; Lesh, Post & Behr, 1987; National Research Council, 2001).

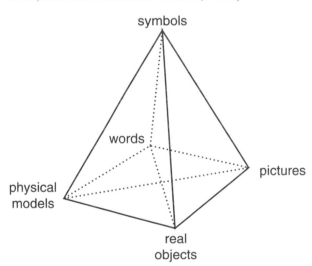

Figure 1: *Ways of representing decimals*

Models for Common and Decimal Fractions

This curriculum uses four main physical models for decimal and common fractions: the area model, the discrete model, the number line, and money. Each model illustrates decimals in a different way. Our goal is for students to become familiar with them all and to move freely among them. We discuss below the benefits and limitations of the different models.

The Area Model. In previous grades, your students worked with common and decimal fractions using area models, mostly rectangles, pattern block figures, and circles. We continue this work here, especially in the lessons *Tenths* and *Hundredths,* where students use base-ten pieces to model decimals. (Strictly speaking, base-ten pieces are a *volume* model for decimals, but pictures of base-ten pieces do approximate an area model.)

The area model is recommended for early work with fractions and decimals (Behr & Post, 1992). Children build on their everyday experiences (cutting toast, sharing pizza, etc.) when they use such models. Many real-life measurement situations (cooking, sewing, carpentry) involve fractions that are similar to fractions modeled with rectangles or circles.

The Discrete Model. In previous grades we also modeled common and decimal fractions with beans, cubes, or other counters. For example, if a dozen eggs is defined to be the unit, then one-half is six eggs, and so on. The number of eggs in one-half of 12 can be determined by separating the eggs into two equal groups and then counting the number of eggs in one group. Models such as this are called *discrete* because the quantities involved are countable. Quantities that are measurable—length, area, volume, mass, time, and so on—are not discrete; mathematicians call them continuous.

Base-ten blocks could be considered a discrete model, since we can find what is represented by each block by counting. Usually, however, when we think of discrete models, we think of distinct objects like beans or eggs.

The Number Line. Another important fraction model is the number line. Fractions on number lines, however, can be hard for some children to understand. For example, in trying to find $\frac{1}{2}$ inch on a ruler, a child might become confused by thinking about $\frac{1}{2}$ of the whole ruler. Another difficulty with the number line is that the end point of an interval is labeled, not the entire interval. So, for example, on a ruler $\frac{1}{2}$ would be marked at a distance of $\frac{1}{2}$ inch from the zero mark, but in a rectangle $\frac{1}{2}$ would be marked in the middle of the half-region. See Figure 2. These contrasting conventions can be confusing. To minimize these difficulties and to provide a real-world context for decimals, we restrict our number line work primarily to measurement situations like the *m, dm, cm, mm* lesson and the *Downhill Racer* lab.

Money. Another common and useful model for decimal fractions is money. Money is a useful model because children are so familiar with it. Children (and adults) have good intuition for situations involving money.

Certain conventions in our way of writing money, however, make its use problematic for beginning instruction in decimals. For example, we conventionally show exactly two decimal places when we write amounts of money (e.g., $4.50, not $4.5); normal decimal notation does not have such a constraint although this notation will be seen on calculator displays. One can also think of an amount like $4.56 in terms of two distinct units, dollars and cents. In this interpretation, the number before the decimal point tells how many dollars, and the number after the decimal point tells how many cents, thus making it harder for students to see the 50 cents as a decimal fraction of a dollar. This is analogous to the use of the colon in writing clock times: the colon divides two distinct units, hours and minutes. Other similar separators are used for feet and inches (4'6") and degrees, minutes, and seconds (47°15'45").

Operations with Decimals

At this point in their mathematical careers, students are developing their conceptual understanding of decimals. The work in this unit—skip counting, measuring, comparing to benchmarks, ordering, translating between various representations—is designed to build this basic understanding. Algorithms for paper-and-pencil addition and subtraction are not introduced until fifth grade, because a focus on standard algorithms at this stage would encourage students to attend to surface features of decimals and could hinder the development of deeper understanding. For most students in fourth grade, it will be more profitable to think through the few problems involving decimals that require computation rather than spending considerable time learning computational procedures.

When students encounter problems that require computations with decimals, urge them to invent their own methods to solve them or use a calculator. If students have a good understanding of the meaning of decimals and a good grasp of the problem situations, then inventing solution methods is feasible and instructive. This approach of developing conceptual understanding before focusing on procedures is consistent with the way we have developed the arithmetic procedures.

Figure 2: *One-half on a ruler vs. one-half of a rectangle*

Metric Units

The names of the metric units are logically constructed. There are three fundamental metric units: the meter (length), the gram (mass), and the second (time). (The liter and many other units are defined in terms of these three.) By combining these basic units with various prefixes, many convenient units of measure are obtained.

The prefixes come either from Latin or Greek. The Greek prefixes are used to indicate multiples of the basic unit; the Latin prefixes indicate subdivisions of the basic unit. So, for example, the Greek *kilo-* (1000) yields kilogram and kilometer, meaning 1000 grams and 1000 meters, respectively; the Latin *milli-* (1000) yields millimeter and milligram, meaning $\frac{1}{1000}$ meter and $\frac{1}{1000}$ gram.

Time is different from length and mass in that metric prefixes are only used for units smaller than one second. Metric units for times longer than a second (a 10-hour day, for example) have never been adopted.

Here are some of the most common metric prefixes and their meanings:

- micro- ($\frac{1}{1,000,000}$)
- milli- ($\frac{1}{1000}$)
- centi- ($\frac{1}{100}$)
- deci- ($\frac{1}{10}$)
- mega- (1,000,000)
- kilo- (1000)
- hecto- (100)
- deka- (10)

As students work with decimals, encourage them to share their strategies and experiences.

Resources

- Ball, D.L. "Halves, Pieces, and Twoths: Constructing Representational Contexts in Teaching Fractions." In T.P. Carpenter, E. Fennema, and T.A. Romberg (Eds.), *Rational Numbers: An Integration of Research.* Lawrence Erlbaum Associates, Hillsdale, NJ, 1993.
- Behr, M.J., and T.R. Post. "Teaching Rational Number and Decimal Concepts." In T. Post (Ed.), *Teaching Mathematics in Grades K–8: Research-Based Methods.* Allyn and Bacon, Boston, 1992.
- Hiebert, J. "Research Report: Decimal Fractions." *Arithmetic Teacher,* 34 (7), pp. 22–23, 1987.
- Hiebert, J., and D. Wearne. "Procedures over Concepts: The Acquisition of Decimal Number Knowledge." In J. Hiebert (Ed.), *Conceptual and Procedural Knowledge: The Case of Mathematics.* Lawrence Erlbaum Associates, Hillsdale, NJ, 1986.
- Hiebert, J., D. Wearne, and S. Taber. "Fourth Graders' Gradual Construction of Decimal Fractions during Instruction Using Different Physical Representations." *Elementary School Journal,* 91 (4), pp. 321–341, 1991.
- Lesh, R., T. Post, and M. Behr. "Representations and Translations among Representation in Mathematics Learning and Problem Solving." In C. Janvier (Ed.), *Problems of Representation in the Teaching and Learning of Mathematics* (Chapter 4). Lawrence Erlbaum Associates, Hillsdale, NJ, and London, 1987.
- National Research Council. "Developing Proficiency with Other Numbers." In *Adding It Up: Helping Children Learn Mathematics.* J. Kilpatrick, J. Swafford, and B. Findell (Eds.). National Academy Press, Washington, DC, 2001.
- Payne, J.N., A.E. Towsley, and D.M. Huinker. "Fractions and Decimals." In J.N. Payne (Ed.), *Mathematics for the Young Child.* National Council of Teachers of Mathematics, Reston, VA, 1990.
- Wearne, D., and J. Hiebert. "A Cognitive Approach to Meaningful Mathematics Instruction: Testing a Local Theory Using Decimal Numbers." *Journal for Research in Mathematics Education,* 19 (5), pp. 371–384, 1988.
- Wearne, D., and J. Hiebert. "Cognitive Changes during Conceptually Based Instruction on Decimal Fractions." *Journal of Educational Psychology,* 81 (4), pp. 507–513, 1989.

Observational Assessment Record

A1 Can students represent decimals using number lines (metersticks) and base-ten pieces?

A2 Can students read and write decimals to hundredths?

A3 Can students skip count by tenths and hundredths?

A4 Can students measure length to the nearest mm, cm, dm, and m?

A5 Can students collect, organize, graph, and analyze data?

A6 Do students demonstrate fluency with the division facts for the 2s and 3s?

A7 _____

Name	A1	A2	A3	A4	A5	A6	A7	Comments
1.								
2.								
3.								
4.								
5.								
6.								
7.								
8.								
9.								
10.								
11.								
12.								
13.								

Name	A1	A2	A3	A4	A5	A6	A7	Comments
14.								
15.								
16.								
17.								
18.								
19.								
20.								
21.								
22.								
23.								
24.								
25.								
26.								
27.								
28.								
29.								
30.								
31.								
32.								

Unit 10

Daily Practice and Problems
Using Decimals

A DPP Menu for Unit 10

Two Daily Practice and Problems (DPP) items are included for each class session listed in the Unit Outline. A scope and sequence chart for the DPP is in the *Teacher Implementation Guide*.

Icons in the Teacher Notes column designate the subject matter of each DPP item. The first item in each class session is always a Bit and the second is either a Task or Challenge. Each item falls into one or more of the categories listed below. A menu of the DPP items for Unit 10 follows.

N Number Sense	Computation	Time	Geometry
D, I, O, P, R–V	H, K, M, N, X	N	F, J, L
Math Facts	$ Money	Measurement	Data
B–D, G, K, M, Q, W, X		A, E, F, I, L, T, V	

Practice and Assessment of the Division Facts

The DPP for this unit continues the systematic strategies-based approach to learning the division facts. This unit practices and assesses the twos and threes. The *Triangle Flash Cards* for these groups are in the *Discovery Assignment Book* and in the *Grade 4 Facts Resource Guide*. A discussion of

the flash cards and how they might be used is in item B of the DPP. A quiz on the twos and threes is provided in item W.

For more information about the distribution and assessment of the math facts, see the TIMS Tutor: *Math Facts* in the *Teacher Implementation Guide*. Also refer to the Daily Practice and Problems Guides in the *Unit Resource Guides* for Units 3 and 9.

Unit 10 Daily Practice and Problems

Students may solve the items individually, in groups, or as a class. The items may also be assigned for homework. The DPPs are also available on the Teacher Resource CD.

Student Questions	Teacher Notes
A **Measure with m or cm?**	**TIMS Bit**
1. List some things that you might measure in meters.	Answers will vary and a wide range should be accepted.
2. List some things that would be easier to measure in cm.	

Triangle Flash Cards: 2s and 3s

With a partner, use your *Triangle Flash Cards* to quiz each other on the division facts for the twos and threes. One partner covers the corner displaying the number in a circle. This covered number will be the answer to a division fact called the quotient. The number in the square is the divisor. Use the two uncovered numbers to solve a division fact.

Separate the used cards into three piles: those facts you know and can answer quickly, those you can figure out with a strategy, and those you need to learn. Make a list of the facts in the last two piles.

Put the cards back into one pile and go through them a second time with your partner. This time, your partner covers the number in the square. This number will now be the quotient. The number in the circle is now the divisor. Use the two uncovered numbers to solve a division fact.

Separate the cards again into three piles. Add the facts in the last two piles to your list. Take the list home to practice.

Circle the facts you know quickly on your *Division Facts I Know* chart.

TIMS Task

The *Triangle Flash Cards: 2s and 3s* are located in the *Discovery Assignment Book* after the Home Practice.

After students sort the cards, encourage them to practice the facts in the last two piles. As the class discusses strategies, emphasize those strategies that are more efficient than others. (See DPP items C and G.)

The Home Practice reminds students to bring home their *Triangle Flash Cards* for the 2s and 3s, and to study only small groups of facts (8–10 facts) at one time.

Inform students when you will give the quiz on the 2s and 3s. This quiz appears in item W.

C **Fact Families for × and ÷**

TIMS Bit

The following four facts belong to the same fact family.

3 × 2 = 6	2 × 3 = 6
6 ÷ 2 = 3	6 ÷ 3 = 2

Solve each pair of related number sentences.

Then give two other facts in the same fact family.

A. 3 × 9 = ? and 27 ÷ 9 = ?

B. 2 × 10 = ? and 20 ÷ 10 = ?

C. 2 × 8 = ? and 16 ÷ 2 = ?

D. 6 × 2 = ? and 12 ÷ 6 = ?

E. 10 × 3 = ? and 30 ÷ 3 = ?

F. 5 × 2 = ? and 10 ÷ 5 = ?

G. 1 × 2 = ? and 2 ÷ 2 = ?

Complete this item orally as a class. One student can solve the given facts and two other students can name each of the other two related facts.

A. 27; 3; 9 × 3 = 27;
   27 ÷ 3 = 9

B. 20; 2; 10 × 2 = 20;
   20 ÷ 2 = 10

C. 16; 8; 8 × 2 = 16;
   16 ÷ 8 = 2

D. 12; 2; 2 × 6 = 12;
   12 ÷ 2 = 6

E. 30; 10; 3 × 10 = 30;
   30 ÷ 10 = 3

F. 10; 2; 2 × 5 = 10;
   10 ÷ 2 = 5

G. 2; 1; 2 × 1 = 2;
   2 ÷ 1 = 2

D **Base-Ten Shorthand**

TIMS Task

Write the following numbers or answers in base-ten shorthand. Use the Fewest Pieces Rule.

A bit is one whole.

A. 777	B. 4096
C. 2735	D. 20 × 2
E. 400 × 3	F. 30 × 3
G. 20 × 90	H. 600 × 3

A.

B.

C.

D.

E.

F.

G.

H.

E **When Does $\frac{1}{4}$ Matter?**

1. Might $\frac{1}{4}$ inch be important if you are building a door?

2. Do you think $\frac{1}{4}$ inch is important when you are measuring the distance you can ride on your bike?

3. Give an example when $\frac{1}{4}$ inch is important. Give an example when it is not.

TIMS Bit

1. Yes.

2. No.

3. Answers will vary.

F **Counting Square Units**

1. How many square millimeters are there in one square centimeter? Use the picture below to help you answer the question.

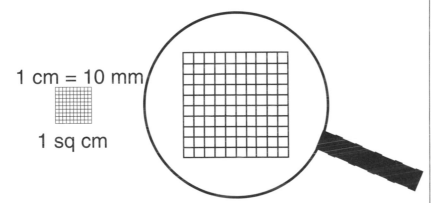

1 cm = 10 mm

1 sq cm

2. How many square centimeters are there in one square meter? It may help if you draw a picture.

TIMS Task

1. 100 square millimeters

2. 10,000 square centimeters

Math Fact Practice

Solve the problem. Then write the other number sentences in the same fact family.

A. $15 \div 5 =$

B. $27 \div 3 =$

C. $16 \div 2 =$

D. $18 \div 2 =$

E. $21 \div 3 =$

F. $24 \div 3 =$

G. $2 \div 2 =$

TIMS Bit

A. 3
$15 \div 3 = 5$
$5 \times 3 = 15$
$3 \times 5 = 15$

B. 9
$27 \div 9 = 3$
$9 \times 3 = 27$
$3 \times 9 = 27$

C. 8
$16 \div 8 = 2$
$8 \times 2 = 16$
$2 \times 8 = 16$

D. 9
$18 \div 9 = 2$
$9 \times 2 = 18$
$2 \times 9 = 18$

E. 7
$21 \div 7 = 3$
$7 \times 3 = 21$
$3 \times 7 = 21$

F. 8
$24 \div 8 = 3$
$8 \times 3 = 24$
$3 \times 8 = 24$

G. 1
$2 \div 1 = 2$
$2 \times 1 = 2$
$1 \times 2 = 2$

Addition, Subtraction, and
Multiplication Practice

Use paper and pencil or mental math to solve the following problems. Be sure to estimate to see if your answers make sense.

1. A. 148 + 779 =   B. 2090 + 793 =

   C. 7084 − 557 = D. 5386 − 737 =

   E. 94 × 7 =   F. 38 × 3 =

   G. 57 × 2 =   H. 4068 − 843 =

   I. 52 × 9 =   J. 87 × 3 =

2. Explain your strategy for Question J.

TIMS Task

1. A. 927
   B. 2883
   C. 6527
   D. 4649
   E. 658
   F. 114
   G. 114
   H. 3225
   I. 468
   J. 261

2. Possible strategy:
   90 × 3 = 270 and
   3 × 3 = 9;
   270 − 9 = 261.

 Number Line Decimals

The picture below shows a piece of a centimeter ruler enlarged. For each letter, write the decimal that matches.

TIMS Bit

A. 0.5 cm
B. 0.9 cm
C. 1.4 cm
D. 8.6 cm
E. 9.1 cm

Line Symmetry

Parts of the pictures below are missing. The dashed lines are lines of symmetry. Copy or trace the pictures on paper and draw in the missing parts.

TIMS Task

 The Price Is Right

Fill in the table. Find the largest second factor so that the product of the two numbers is close to the target number without going over the target number. The first has been filled in for you.

Factor 1	Factor 2	Target Number	Left Over
5	7	38	3
3		28	
2		17	
7		25	
6		20	
9		48	
4		13	
5		12	

TIMS Bit

Students find the largest one-digit number that will provide a product that does not go over the target number. Students practice division facts by solving problems in which the division does not come out evenly.

Factor 1	Factor 2	Target Number	Left Over
5	7	38	3
3	9	28	1
2	8	17	1
7	3	25	4
6	3	20	2
9	5	48	3
4	3	13	1
5	2	12	2

Measuring Angles

You will need a ruler and a protractor to do these problems.

1. Draw a triangle. Make one angle 38°.

2. Draw a quadrilateral. Make one angle 125°.

3. Draw a hexagon. Make one angle 70°.

TIMS Task

Shapes will vary.

1.

38°

2.
125°

3.

70°

M **Multiplying with Zeros**

A. 80 × 20 =   B. 40 × 3 =

C. 3000 × 40 =   D. 20 × 500 =

E. 50 × 30 =   F. 600 × 2 =

G. 0 × 20 =   H. 10 × 30 =

TIMS Bit

A. 1600
B. 120
C. 120,000
D. 10,000
E. 1500
F. 1200
G. 0
H. 300

Time

1 day = 24 hours

1 hour = 60 minutes

1 minute = 60 seconds

1 week = 7 days

1. 5 hours = ? minutes

2. 4 weeks = ? days

3. 3 days = ? hours

4. $\frac{1}{2}$ hour = ? minutes

5. $\frac{1}{4}$ day = ? hours

6. $\frac{1}{10}$ minute = ? seconds

7. 360 minutes = ? hours

8. 42 days = ? weeks

TIMS Challenge

1. 300 minutes

2. 28 days

3. 72 hours

4. 30 minutes

5. 6 hours

6. 6 seconds

7. 6 hours

8. 6 weeks

Skip Counting

1. Skip count by dimes to $2.00.
   Start like this: $0.10, $0.20, $0.30 . . .

2. Skip count by tenths to 2.
   Start like this: 0.1, 0.2, 0.3 . . .

3. Skip count by quarters to $5.00.
   Start like this: $0.25, $0.50, $0.75 . . .

4. Skip count by 0.25 (twenty-five hundredths) to 5. Start like this: 0.25, 0.50, 0.75 . . .

TIMS Bit

In Lesson 4, students may scale their graphs for *Downhill Racer* with intervals of 0.25 or 0.1. This item helps prepare students for this task.

Be sure students say the numbers accurately. For Question 1, for example, they should begin, "10 cents, 20 cents . . . ." For Question 2, they should begin, "one-tenth, two-tenths . . . ."

P **Skip Counting by Tenths and Hundredths**

TIMS Task

Be sure students read the numbers accurately. For example, in Question 1 students should begin, "one-tenth, two-tenths, three-tenths, etc."

1. Use a calculator to skip count by tenths. Skip count by tenths from 0 to 2.

   Press:

   Say the numbers quietly to yourself.

The keystrokes listed work with most calculators that have the constant feature. Test your calculator to make sure that these keystrokes are appropriate for the model you use. If your calculator has the constant feature, each time you press the equal sign in the keystroke sequence for Question 1, for example, the constant number (0.1) and the constant operation (addition) are repeated.

2. Skip count by hundredths from 0 to one-tenth.

   Press:

   Say the numbers quietly to yourself.

3. Skip count by tenths from 5 to 7.

   Press:

   Say the numbers quietly to yourself.

4. Skip count by hundredths from 2 to 2.1.

   Press: 2 + . 0 1 = =

   Say the numbers quietly to yourself.

More Fact Families for × and ÷

The following four facts are in the same fact family.

$4 \times 3 = 12$ $3 \times 4 = 12$

$12 \div 3 = 4$ $12 \div 4 = 3$

Solve each pair of related number sentences. Then give two other facts in the same fact family.

A. $7 \times 2 = ?$ and $14 \div 7 = ?$

B. $2 \times 3 = ?$ and $6 \div 2 = ?$

C. $3 \times 8 = ?$ and $24 \div 3 = ?$

D. $6 \times 3 = ?$ and $18 \div 3 = ?$

E. $4 \times 2 = ?$ and $8 \div 4 = ?$

F. $3 \times 8 = ?$ and $24 \div 8 = ?$

G. $3 \times 1 = ?$ and $3 \div 1 = ?$

A. 14; 2; $2 \times 7 = 14$; $14 \div 2 = 7$

B. 6; 3; $3 \times 2 = 6$; $6 \div 3 = 2$

C. 24; 8; $8 \times 3 = 24$; $24 \div 8 = 3$

D. 18; 6; $3 \times 6 = 18$; $18 \div 6 = 3$

E. 8; 2; $2 \times 4 = 8$; $8 \div 2 = 4$

F. 24; 3; $8 \times 3 = 24$; $24 \div 3 = 8$

G. 3; 3; $1 \times 3 = 3$; $3 \div 3 = 1$

R **Ordering Decimals**

TIMS Task

1. Draw each of the following numbers in base-ten shorthand. The flat is one whole. Then put the numbers in order from smallest to largest:

   0.4   0.39   0.41   0.5   1.00

2. Draw each of the following numbers in base-ten shorthand. The flat is one whole. Then put these numbers in order from smallest to largest:

   0.09   0.8   1.0   0.27   0.01

1.

0.39, 0.4, 0.41, 0.5, 1.00

2.

0.01, 0.09, 0.27, 0.8, 1.0

Write a Decimal

1. Write a decimal:

   A. between 7 and 8

   B. between 1 and 2

   C. just a little bigger than 4

   D. just a little less than 2

   E. between $\frac{1}{2}$ and 0.8

   F. between 5 and 5.5

2. Explain your strategy for Question E.

TIMS Bit

Answers will vary.

 Which Length Is Longer?

1. Use a meterstick to help you answer the following.

   (Bits and skinnies might help, too. Remember, one bit is one centimeter long. One skinny is 10 cm or 1 decimeter long.) Which is longer:

   A. 2 cm or 11 mm?

   B. 32 mm or 3 cm?

   C. 5 dm or 45 cm?

   D. 2 m or 180 cm?

   E. 3 dm or 300 mm?

   F. 87 cm or 8 dm?

2. Choose one of the questions and explain your strategy for solving it.

TIMS Task

1. A. 2 cm
   B. 32 mm
   C. 5 dm
   D. 2 m
   E. These two are equal.
   F. 87 cm
2. Answers will vary.

Smallest, Largest, and In-Between

For the following base-ten shorthand, the flat is one whole.

1. □□□ ////

2. □□□□ ///

3. □ // □ // □ // □

4. □□ /// □□

   A. Which is the smallest?

   B. Which is the largest?

   C. Which are equal?

   D. Write numbers for each and put them in order from smallest to largest. (The flat is one whole.)

TIMS Bit

A. 1

B. 3

C. 2 and 4

D. 3.4, 4.3, 4.3, 4.6

V **Metric Conversions**

Change each of these lengths to meters.
(*Hint:* Think of metersticks, skinnies, and bits.)

  A. 327 cm   B. 405 cm

  C. 5 cm   D. 87 cm

  E. 10 dm   F. 24 dm

Change each of these lengths to centimeters.

  G. 1.1 m   H. 1.01 m

  I. 4 dm   J. 4.1 dm

  K. 3.27 m   L. 0.4 dm

TIMS Task

A. 3.27 m	B. 4.05 m
C. 0.05 m	D. 0.87 m
E. 1 m	F. 2.4 m
G. 110 cm	H. 101 cm
I. 40 cm	J. 41 cm
K. 327 cm	L. 4 cm

Quiz on 2s and 3s Division Facts

A. $8 \div 2 =$ B. $30 \div 3 =$

C. $16 \div 2 =$ D. $9 \div 3 =$

E. $12 \div 2 =$ F. $21 \div 3 =$

G. $15 \div 3 =$ H. $4 \div 2 =$

I. $10 \div 2 =$ J. $27 \div 3 =$

K. $14 \div 2 =$ L. $12 \div 3 =$

M. $6 \div 3 =$ N. $24 \div 3 =$

O. $2 \div 1 =$ P. $18 \div 3 =$

Q. $18 \div 2 =$ R. $3 \div 3 =$

S. $20 \div 2 =$

TIMS Bit

We recommend 2 minutes for this quiz. Allow students to change pens after the time is up and complete the remaining problems in a different color.

After students take the quiz, have them update their *Division Facts I Know* charts. Since students learned the division facts through work with fact families, it is likely that the student who answers $12 \div 2$ correctly also knows the answer to $12 \div 6$. To make sure, however, ask students to write a related division fact for each of the facts on the quiz (except $9 \div 3$ and $4 \div 2$). A student who answers a given fact correctly and also writes the correct related fact can circle both facts on the chart.

A. 4		B. 10	
C. 8		D. 3	
E. 6		F. 7	
G. 5		H. 2	
I. 5		J. 9	
K. 7		L. 4	
M. 2		N. 8	
O. 2		P. 6	
Q. 9		R. 1	
S. 10			

 Dividing It Up

$26 \div 8 =$? Write a story for $26 \div 8$. Then draw a picture. Include any remainder in your picture.

TIMS Task

3 R2

Lesson 1

m, dm, cm, mm

Lesson Overview

Estimated Class Sessions

2

Students measure objects in the classroom to the nearest meter, decimeter, centimeter, and millimeter. Students also use decimal notation to record measurements through hundredths of a meter.

Key Content

- Measuring lengths in metric units (m, dm, cm, and mm).
- Representing decimals using base-ten pieces and number lines (metersticks).
- Reading and writing decimals to the hundredths.
- Understanding place value for decimals.
- Choosing the most appropriate unit of measure to solve problems.

Key Vocabulary

- centimeter
- decimal
- decimeter
- hundredth
- meter
- millimeter
- nearest tenth

Math Facts

DPP items B and C provide practice with division facts. Task D provides practice with base-ten shorthand and multiplying with multiples of 10.

Homework

1. Assign *Questions 1–2* in the Homework section of the *m, dm, cm, mm* Activity Pages after Part 1.
2. Assign *Question 3* in the Homework section of the *m, dm, cm, mm* Activity Pages after Part 3.
3. Assign Parts 1 and 2 of the Home Practice.

Assessment

1. Use the *Observational Assessment Record* to document students' abilities to measure length to the nearest mm, cm, dm, and m.
2. Set up a performance assessment task in which students measure specified objects.

Materials List

Supplies and Copies

Student	Teacher
Supplies for Each Student • 1 meter of string • centimeter ruler • envelope for storing flash cards **Supplies for Each Student Group** • 1 or 2 metersticks • about 10 skinnies and 10 bits	**Supplies** • masking tape
Copies	**Copies/Transparencies** • 1 transparency of *Class Measurement Tables* (*Discovery Assignment Book* Page 163) • 1 copy of *Observational Assessment Record* to be used throughout this unit (*Unit Resource Guide* Pages 13–14)

All blackline masters including assessment, transparency, and DPP masters are also on the Teacher Resource CD.

Student Books

m, dm, cm, mm (*Student Guide* Pages 270–275)
Triangle Flash Cards: 2s (*Discovery Assignment Book* Page 159)
Triangle Flash Cards: 3s (*Discovery Assignment Book* Page 161)
Class Measurement Tables (*Discovery Assignment Book* Page 163)
Measure Hunt (*Discovery Assignment Book* Pages 165–166)

Daily Practice and Problems and Home Practice

DPP items A–D (*Unit Resource Guide* Pages 16–18)
Home Practice Parts 1–2 (*Discovery Assignment Book* Page 155)

Note: Classrooms whose pacing differs significantly from the suggested pacing of the units should use the Math Facts Calendar in Section 4 of the *Facts Resource Guide* to ensure students receive the complete math facts program.

Assessment Tools

Observational Assessment Record (*Unit Resource Guide* Pages 13–14)

Daily Practice and Problems

Suggestions for using the DPPs are on page 37.

A. Bit: Measure with m or cm? (URG p. 16)

1. List some things that you might measure in meters.
2. List some things that would be easier to measure in cm.

B. Task: *Triangle Flash Cards: 2s and 3s*
(URG p. 17)

With a partner, use your *Triangle Flash Cards* to quiz each other on the division facts for the twos and threes. One partner covers the corner displaying the number in a circle. This covered number will be the answer to a division fact called the quotient. The number in the square is the divisor. Use the two uncovered numbers to solve a division fact.

Separate the used cards into three piles: those facts you know and can answer quickly, those you can figure out with a strategy, and those you need to learn. Make a list of the facts in the last two piles.

Put the cards back into one pile and go through them a second time with your partner. This time, your partner covers the number in the square. This number will now be the quotient. The number in the circle is now the divisor. Use the two uncovered numbers to solve a division fact.

Separate the cards again into three piles. Add the facts in the last two piles to your list. Take the list home to practice.

Circle the facts you know quickly on your *Division Facts I Know* chart.

C. Bit: Fact Families for × and ÷
(URG p. 18)

The following four facts belong to the same fact family.

$3 \times 2 = 6$ $2 \times 3 = 6$

$6 \div 2 = 3$ $6 \div 3 = 2$

Solve each pair of related number sentences.

Then give two other facts in the same fact family.

A. $3 \times 9 = ?$ and $27 \div 9 = ?$

B. $2 \times 10 = ?$ and $20 \div 10 = ?$

C. $2 \times 8 = ?$ and $16 \div 2 = ?$

D. $6 \times 2 = ?$ and $12 \div 6 = ?$

E. $10 \times 3 = ?$ and $30 \div 3 = ?$

F. $5 \times 2 = ?$ and $10 \div 5 = ?$

G. $1 \times 2 = ?$ and $2 \div 2 = ?$

D. Task: Base-Ten Shorthand
(URG p. 18)

Write the following numbers or answers in base-ten shorthand. Use the Fewest Pieces Rule.

A bit is one whole.

A. 777   B. 4096

C. 2735   D. 20×2

E. 400×3 F. 30×3

G. 20×90 H. 600×3

Before the Activity

Place a piece of tape on a wall or door 1 meter from the floor and another piece 2 meters from the floor in a location visible to all students. (These will be used for estimating heights using the benchmarks 1 m and 2 m.) Cut a piece of string one meter long for each student or have students measure and cut strings at the end of Part 1.

Teaching the Activity

This activity leads students through measuring the same objects several times with progressively smaller units. Students are led to see that it is usually unsatisfactory to measure small objects such as paper clips or pencils to the nearest whole meter. When we use too large a measure, we get very little useful information. If I tell you how many miles long my living room is to the nearest whole mile, you don't learn much. If I tell you how many light-years it is to the nearest whole light-year from Chicago to Paducah, that doesn't help much either. Choosing the appropriate unit of measure, for example, miles for Chicago to Paducah and feet for a living room, helps make sense of the measurement.

Part 1 Meters and Decimeters

The Meters section of the *m, dm, cm, mm* Activity Pages in the *Student Guide* introduces measuring to the nearest meter. In **Question 4,** the class completes a data table in the *Discovery Assignment Book* with measurements of objects in the classroom as shown in Figure 3. Record students' measurements on a transparency of the *Class Measurement Tables* Activity Page.

In the later parts of this activity, we measure these same objects using smaller units. Create different class data tables each time instead of adding columns to the first table. If you record the measurement of a door's height as 2 meters and then record it as 19 decimeters in the same table, students may mistakenly think the height is 2 meters 19 decimeters.

> ### TIMS Tip
>
> To avoid students grouping around certain objects or wandering about looking for objects to measure, make a list of classroom objects that students can measure. Assign groups of students to measure certain objects.

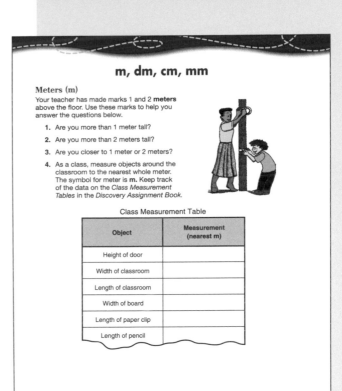

Student Guide - page 270 (Answers on p. 41)

Measurements to the Nearest Meter Data Table

Object	Measurement (nearest m)
Height of door	2
Width of classroom	8
Length of classroom	14
Width of board	5
Length of paper clip	0
Length of pencil	0

Figure 3: *Measurements to the nearest meter data table*

Name _____   Date _____

Class Measurement Tables

To the Nearest Meter	
Object	Measurement (nearest m)
Height of Door	
Width of Classroom	
Length of Classroom	
Width of Board	
Length of Paper Clip	
Length of Pencil	

To the Nearest Decimeter	
Object	Measurement (nearest dm)
Height of Door	
Width of Classroom	
Length of Classroom	
Width of Board	
Length of Paper Clip	
Length of Pencil	

To the Nearest Centimeter

Object	Measurement (nearest cm)
Height of Door	
Width of Classroom	
Length of Classroom	
Width of Board	
Length of Paper Clip	
Length of Pencil	

m, dm, cm, mm   DAB • Grade 4 • Unit 10 • Lesson 1 **163**

Discovery Assignment Book - page 163 *(Answers on p. 44)*

5. Jackie measured her calculator to the nearest meter and found it to be 0 meters long. What does this measurement (0 m) tell you? What unit would give you a better measurement for this length?

6. Sometimes it is good enough to measure to the nearest whole meter. Sometimes it is not. Usually, it does not make sense to measure a calculator to the nearest meter. List two things that probably should not be measured to the nearest meter.

7. List two things that you would measure to the nearest meter.

Decimeters (dm)

8. How many skinnies can you line up on a meterstick? Line them up along a meterstick to find out.

9. The length of one skinny is a **deci**meter. The symbol for decimeter is **dm**. How many dm are in 1 meter? How many dm are in $\frac{1}{2}$ meter?

10. A decimeter is $\frac{1}{10}$ of a meter. What do you think **deci-** means?

11. As a class, measure the objects in the table from Question 4 again. This time, measure to the nearest whole decimeter. Make a new table for this data like the one shown below.

Class Measurement Table

Object	Measurement (nearest dm)
Height of door	
Width of classroom	
Length of classroom	

m, dm, cm, mm   SG • Grade 4 • Unit 10 • Lesson 1 **271**

Student Guide - page 271 *(Answers on p. 41)*

Question 8 asks how many skinnies you can line up along a meterstick. Ask:

- *If a decimeter is one-tenth, then what is one whole?* Ten decimeters make a meter.
- *If a skinny is one-tenth of a whole unit, what base-ten piece represents the whole?* Ten skinnies make a flat.

Question 11 asks students to remeasure objects they measured to the nearest meter, but this time to the nearest decimeter using metersticks and skinnies. Record this data in the appropriate data table on the *Class Measurement Tables* Activity Page. Discuss the differences between the two tables.

Another way to foster intuitions about length is to identify reference lengths for different units of measure. For example, when students think of a meter, they could think of the distance between the floor and a doorknob. Ask:

- *What object do you think of when I say, how long is a centimeter?*
- *A millimeter?*
- *A decimeter?*
- *A meter?*

You can list ideas for "unit reference lengths" on a bulletin board.

At this point in the lesson, you can assign *Questions 1–2* in the Homework section of the *m, dm, cm, mm* Activity Pages in the *Student Guide.* They are designed to help students develop intuitions about the metric system and the length of a meter. Students can use their meter-length strings or regular metersticks to measure.

Content Note

The **decimeter** is a metric unit not commonly used in the United States. We include it here for completeness and because sometimes it is the best unit to use. The centimeter is more commonly used for small lengths; however, even whole centimeters are too large for tiny lengths like the thickness of a penny, the thickness of a piece of hair, or the thickness of a compact disc. For these we use millimeters or even smaller units.

Part 2 Centimeters and Millimeters

Students measure the objects again, this time to the nearest centimeter using metersticks and bits. Display the results in another class data table. A comparison of the three tables should be instructive.

Use the Centimeters section of the *m, dm, cm, mm* Activity Pages to direct your discussion.

After completing *Question 16,* you might ask students why they think they are not asked in the Centimeters part of the Activity Pages to measure the objects to the nearest millimeter. They should see that in most cases it may be difficult and not necessary to measure larger objects to the nearest millimeter. See the TIMS Tutor: *Estimation, Accuracy, and Error* in the *Teacher Implementation Guide* for more information.

After students answer *Question 22,* ask:

- *How would you record 1 decimeter as part of a meter?* (0.1 m)

- *How would you record 1 centimeter as part of a meter?* (0.01 m)

- *How would you record 1 millimeter as part of a meter?* (0.001 m)

Discuss both decimal and common fractions. The *m, dm, cm, mm* Activity Pages reinforce and build upon this discussion.

Content Note

Reading Decimals. The symbols *4.3* are usually read as "four and three-tenths" or "four point three." Either reading is correct, but we prefer the former at this stage because it makes the connection with fractions explicit. We want students to think of decimals as fractions, not merely as strings of symbols.

Journal Prompt

Most door handles are about one meter from the floor. Why do you think this is? Can you think of another example of something that is almost always placed at the same height?

---

12. John measured a paper clip to the nearest decimeter. He found it to be 0 decimeters long. What information does this measurement tell you? What unit would give you a better measurement for a paper clip?

13. Sometimes it is good enough to measure to the nearest whole decimeter. Sometimes it is not. List two things that should be measured to the nearest decimeter.

Centimeters (cm)
A **cent**ury is 100 years; a **cent**ennial is a 100-year anniversary; a **cent**ipede is said to have 100 legs. What do you think **cent-** means?

A **cent**imeter is $\frac{1}{100}$ of a meter and a **cent** is $\frac{1}{100}$ of a dollar. In other words, there are 100 centimeters in a meter and 100 cents in a dollar.

14. How many bits can you line up along a meterstick? How did you decide?

15. How long is a bit?

16. As a class, measure the objects from Question 4 again. This time, measure to the nearest whole centimeter. Make a new table for this data like the one shown below.

17. List two things it makes sense to measure to the nearest whole centimeter. List two things it does not make sense to measure in centimeters.

18. Find an object that measures less than 1 centimeter.

Class Measurement Table

Object	Measurement (nearest cm)
Height of door	
Width of classroom	
Length of classroom	

272   SG · Grade 4 · Unit 10 · Lesson 1   m, dm, cm, mm

Student Guide - page 272 (Answers on p. 42)

Millimeters (mm)
If you look at a meterstick very carefully, you will see little spaces between short lines. Each one of these spaces is a millimeter.

19. There are 1000 **milli**meters in a meter. What do you think **milli-** means?

20. How many millimeters are in a centimeter?

21. How many millimeters are in a decimeter? How did you decide?

22. People generally use millimeters to measure very short lengths. Give an example of when it would make sense to measure in millimeters.

Measuring with Metersticks, Skinnies, and Bits
John measured the length of the board in his classroom. First, he used two metersticks. He saw that less than half of a third meterstick would fit. John said, "To the nearest whole meter, this length is 2 meters."

m, dm, cm, mm   SG · Grade 4 · Unit 10 · Lesson 1   **273**

Student Guide - page 273 (Answers on p. 42)

Next, John put down four skinnies. John said, "Each meterstick is ten decimeters, and each skinny is one decimeter long. I have two metersticks and four skinnies. So, to the nearest decimeter, this length is 24 whole decimeters."

John still had a little space left. He put down one bit. One bit is one centimeter long.

Mrs. Dewey complimented John's work: "John, you have done a terrific job. You have found the length of the board using the fewest pieces. You can write down this measurement using decimals. How many metersticks did you use?" "Two," said John.

Mrs. Dewey wrote "2." on the board. "Each decimeter is one-tenth of a meter. How many skinnies did you use?" "Four," said John.

Mrs. Dewey wrote "2.4" on the board. "Each centimeter is one-hundredth of a meter. How many bits did you use?" "One," said John.

Mrs. Dewey wrote "2.41" on the board. "This number is read two and forty-one hundredths." John showed 2.41 m with two metersticks, four skinnies, and 1 bit.

John continued to measure objects around the room to the nearest hundredth of a meter. For example, Mrs. Dewey had a life-size poster of a professional basketball player on the wall. John decided to measure the height of this player. He used 1 meterstick, 9 skinnies, and 8 bits. John wrote "1.98 meters" for this measurement. That told him the player's height was 1 meter, 9 decimeters, and 8 centimeters.

23. John wrote the following measurements on his paper. He used the fewest pieces for each measurement. How many metersticks, skinnies, and bits did John use for each measurement?
    A. 3.45 m
    B. 0.59 m
    C. 2.70 m
    D. 2.07 m

Student Guide - page 274 (Answers on p. 43)

Part 3 *Measure Hunt*
Use the Measuring with Metersticks, Skinnies, and Bits section in the *Student Guide* to introduce a slight variation of the Fewest Pieces Rule using bits, skinnies, and metersticks. In measuring, students should first use as many metersticks as possible, then as many skinnies as possible, and then as many bits as possible. This will result in measuring with the fewest number of pieces.

After completing *Question 23* in the *Student Guide,* students complete the *Measure Hunt* Activity Pages in the *Discovery Assignment Book.* Students will measure objects in the room to the nearest hundredth of a meter. Each group of students will need 2 metersticks, 8–10 skinnies, 10 bits, and the *Measure Hunt* Activity Pages. First, students measure using metersticks, skinnies, and bits and record the data on Table 1. Then students measure other objects using only metersticks and record the data on Table 2.

Name _____ Date _____

Measure Hunt

Find four lengths in the classroom using the rules in the table below. Use the fewest pieces possible when you measure. Use metersticks to measure meters. Use skinnies to measure decimeters. Use bits to measure centimeters. Then complete the table. An example is done for you.

Table 1

Rule	Object	Number of m	dm	cm	Length (nearest 0.01 m)
Between 1 and 2 m	Height of cabinet	1	2	0	1.20
Between 1 and 1.5 m					
Between 0.5 and 1 m					
Between 0.5 and 0.8 m					
Between 0.55 and 0.75 m					

Discovery Assignment Book - page 165 (Answers on p. 45)

Name _____ Date _____

Find five lengths in the classroom using the rules in the table below. Use metersticks to measure the lengths. Then complete the table.

Table 2

Rule	Object	Number of m	dm	cm	Length (nearest 0.01 m)
Between 1 and 2 m					
Between 1 and 1.5 m					
Between 0.5 and 1 m					
Between 0.6 and 0.9 m					
Between 0.40 and 0.65 m					

Discovery Assignment Book - page 166 (Answers on p. 45)

Math Facts

- DPP Task B reminds students to practice the division facts for the twos and threes. Bit C provides practice with fact families. Task D provides practice writing numbers in base-ten shorthand as well as multiplying with multiples of 10.

- Part 1 of the Home Practice reminds students to practice division facts for the twos and threes using their *Triangle Flash Cards*.

Homework and Practice

- Assign *Questions 1–2* in the Homework section on the *m, dm, cm, mm* Activity Pages after Part 1. Assign *Question 3* after Part 3. Students will need their meter strings to help them measure.

- DPP Bit A asks students to consider how to choose appropriate units of measure.

- Assign Part 2 of the Home Practice. It includes computation, rounding, and estimation practice.

Answers for Part 2 of the Home Practice are in the Answer Key at the end of this lesson and at the end of this unit.

Assessment

- Observe whether students can measure to the nearest mm, cm, dm, and m. Record your observations on the *Observational Assessment Record*.

- Another way to find out whether students can measure accurately is by setting up a performance assessment. First, identify standard objects that all students can measure simultaneously. For example, ask students to measure any of the following:

  1. the length and width of their desks
  2. the length and width of their *Student Guides*
  3. the length of a standard paper clip
  4. the length and width of a piece of paper
  5. the length of a chalkboard or a bulletin board

     Let students find the appropriate unit of length for each object and then have them carry out the measurements.

Dear Family Member:

In everyday life in the United States, we are slowly moving toward regular use of metric measurements. In scientific life, however, the metric system is already here. To succeed in a technological world, students need to know the metric system. This homework assignment will help your child become aware of the increasing use of metric units.

Thank you for your cooperation.

We often use customary units of measure (inches, pints, pounds, and so on) in everyday life. And there are many times we use metric units of measure (centimeters, liters, grams, and so on).

1. Look for metric units in the newspaper, on labels, and on other household items. Make a list showing what the unit is and what is being measured. If you can, bring in the item with the measurement on it.

2. A. Cut a piece of string 1 meter long.
   B. Carry your meter string with you all the time for one week.
   C. Estimate the length of various objects to the nearest meter. Then use your meter string to measure the objects to the nearest meter. Make a table showing the objects, your estimates, and your measurements.

3. Go on a measure hunt in your home. Look for objects that are between the specified lengths. Complete a data table like this one. (*Hint*: Half of your string is 0.5 m.)

Rule	Object
Between 1 and 2 m	
Between 1 and 1.5 m	
Between 0.5 and 1 m	

m, dm, cm, mm   SG • Grade 4 • Unit 10 • Lesson 1 **275**

Student Guide - page 275 (Answers on p. 43)

Name _____ Date _____

Unit 10 Home Practice

PART 1 *Triangle Flash Cards: 2s and 3s*
Study for the quiz on the division facts for the 2s and 3s. Take home your *Triangle Flash Cards* and your list of facts you need to study.

Here's how to use the flash cards. Ask a family member to choose one flash card at a time. He or she should cover the corner containing either the square or the circle. This number will be the answer to a division fact. Solve a division problem with the two uncovered numbers.

Your teacher will tell you when the quiz on the 2s and 3s will be. Remember to concentrate on one small group of facts each night—about 8 to 10 facts. Also, remember to study only those facts you cannot answer correctly and quickly.

PART 2 **Missing Numbers and Big Numbers**

1. What number must *n* be to make each number sentence true? After you have decided on a number for *n*, check your work by multiplying.
   A. $n \times 20 = 80$ B. $300 \times n = 1800$ C. $90 \times n = 2700$

   D. $50 \times n = 10,000$ E. $n \times 50 = 1500$ F. $70 \times n = 210$

2. A. Write the following numbers in order from smallest to largest.
      45,676   54,673   45,788   48,654   47,998   45,089

   B. Round 48,654 to the nearest thousand.

   C. Round 45,089 to the nearest hundred.

3. Use convenient numbers to estimate the answers to the following problems. Record number sentences to show your thinking.
   A. 608,965 + 28,696   B. 2,657,223 + 3,908,700   C. 378,904 − 99,645

USING DECIMALS   DAB • Grade 4 • Unit 10 **155**

Discovery Assignment Book - page 155 (Answers on p. 44)

Discovery Assignment Book - page 159

Discovery Assignment Book - page 161

- Students should estimate lengths throughout this unit. One type of estimate is a judgment whether an object is longer or shorter than some benchmark: Is your desk wider than 30 cm? How do you know? Is your arm longer or shorter than one meter? How do you know? Another type of estimate is a rough judgment of a length: Estimate the length of your foot in decimeters. Now estimate your foot in centimeters. Would it make sense to estimate the length of your foot in millimeters? Checking estimates by measuring will improve both estimation and measurement skills.

- Ask students to draw a line two decimeters long. Then ask them to attach a 3 cm line and a 5 millimeter line to it. What is the total length of the line in millimeters? Centimeters? Decimeters? Repeat for other lengths.

- What is 17 mm plus 4 cm? (It is not 21 anything.) Draw a 17 mm line and then attach a 4 cm line to it. Students can write their answer in mm and in cm. Repeat for other lengths.

At a Glance

Math Facts and Daily Practice and Problems

DPP items B and C provide practice with division facts. Task D provides practice with base-ten shorthand and multiplying with multiples of 10. Bit A requires consideration of appropriate units of measure.

Part 1. Meters and Decimeters

1. Place a piece of tape on a door or wall 1 meter (m) above the floor and a second piece 2 meters above the floor.
2. Students determine if their heights are closer to 1 m or 2 m. (*Questions 1–3* in the *Student Guide*)
3. Students measure objects to the nearest m. (*Question 4*)
4. Students record their measurements on the *Class Measurement Tables* Activity Page in the *Discovery Assignment Book*.
5. Discuss when it is appropriate to measure to the nearest meter. (*Questions 5–6*)
6. Students line up 10 skinnies along a meterstick. (*Question 8*)
7. Discuss the prefix *deci-* and the word decimeter (dm). (*Questions 9–10*)
8. Students measure objects to the nearest dm. A class data table is created. (*Question 11*)
9. Discuss when it is appropriate to measure to the nearest decimeter. (*Questions 12–13*)

Part 2. Centimeters and Millimeters

1. Discuss the prefix *centi-* and the word centimeter (cm).
2. Students determine that they can line up 100 bits along a meter. (*Questions 14–15*)
3. Students measure objects to the nearest cm. A class table is created. (*Question 16*)
4. Discuss when it is appropriate to measure to the nearest centimeter. (*Questions 17–18*)
5. Discuss the prefix *milli-* and the use of millimeters (mm). (*Questions 19–22*)

Part 3. *Measure Hunt*

1. Students read and discuss the Measuring with Metersticks, Skinnies, and Bits section in the *Student Guide*. Discuss John's measurements, the Fewest Pieces Rule, and how to use decimals to record measurements. Complete *Question 23*.
2. Students use the *Measure Hunt* Activity Pages in the *Discovery Assignment Book* to find objects of certain lengths using metersticks, skinnies, and bits. They fill in the tables.

Homework

1. Assign *Questions 1–2* in the Homework section of the *m, dm, cm, mm* Activity Pages after Part 1.
2. Assign *Question 3* in the Homework section of the *m, dm, cm, mm* Activity Pages after Part 3.
3. Assign Parts 1 and 2 of the Home Practice.

Assessment

1. Use the *Observational Assessment Record* to document students' abilities to measure length to the nearest mm, cm, dm, and m.
2. Set up a performance assessment task in which students measure specified objects.

At a Glance

Extension

1. Have students estimate lengths throughout the unit.
2. Have students draw a line in dm, then add a line drawn in cm, and a line drawn in mm. Then, tell the total length in m, dm, cm, and mm.
3. Challenge students to solve problems such as *What is 17 mm plus 4 cm?*

Answer Key is on pages 41–45.

Notes:

Student Guide (p. 270)

m, dm, cm, mm

1. Yes

2. No

3. Answers will vary.

4. A sample class data table follows.*

Measurements to the Nearest Meter

Object	Measurement (nearest m)
Height of door	2
Width of classroom	8
Length of classroom	14
Width of board	5
Length of paper clip	0
Length of pencil	0

Student Guide (p. 271)

5. A measurement of 0 m tells you the object is less than 0.5 m long. Centimeters or decimeters are more appropriate units.

6. Two possible answers: a pencil and the diameter of a nickel.

7. Two possible answers: The length of a room and the height of a building.

8. 10*

9. 10 dm = 1 m; 5 dm = $\frac{1}{2}$ m

10. $\frac{1}{10}$

11. A sample class data table follows.*

Measurements to the Nearest Decimeter

Object	Measurement (nearest dm)
Height of door	22
Width of classroom	84
Length of classroom	137
Width of board	49
Length of paper clip	0
Length of pencil	1

m, dm, cm, mm

Meters (m)
Your teacher has made marks 1 and 2 **meters** above the floor. Use these marks to help you answer the questions below.

1. Are you more than 1 meter tall?
2. Are you more than 2 meters tall?
3. Are you closer to 1 meter or 2 meters?
4. As a class, measure objects around the classroom to the nearest whole meter. The symbol for meter is **m.** Keep track of the data on the *Class Measurement Tables* in the *Discovery Assignment Book*.

Class Measurement Table

Object	Measurement (nearest m)
Height of door	
Width of classroom	
Length of classroom	
Width of board	
Length of paper clip	
Length of pencil	

270   SG • Grade 4 • Unit 10 • Lesson 1   m, dm, cm, mm

Student Guide - page 270

5. Jackie measured her calculator to the nearest meter and found it to be 0 meters long. What does this measurement (0 m) tell you? What unit would give you a better measurement for this length?

6. Sometimes it is good enough to measure to the nearest whole meter. Sometimes it is not. Usually, it does not make sense to measure a calculator to the nearest meter. List two things that probably should not be measured to the nearest meter.

7. List two things that you would measure to the nearest meter.

Decimeters (dm)
8. How many skinnies can you line up on a meterstick? Line them up along a meterstick to find out.

9. The length of one skinny is a **decimeter**. The symbol for decimeter is **dm.** How many dm are in 1 meter? How many dm are in $\frac{1}{2}$ meter?

10. A decimeter is $\frac{1}{10}$ of a meter. What do you think **deci-** means?

11. As a class, measure the objects in the table from Question 4 again. This time, measure to the nearest whole decimeter. Make a new table for this data like the one shown below.

Class Measurement Table

Object	Measurement (nearest dm)
Height of door	
Width of classroom	
Length of classroom	

m, dm, cm, mm   SG • Grade 4 • Unit 10 • Lesson 1   271

Student Guide - page 271

*Answers and/or discussion are included in the Lesson Guide.

Student Guide - page 272

Student Guide - page 273

*Answers and/or discussion are included in the Lesson Guide.

Student Guide (p. 272)

12. The paper clip is less than 0.5 dm long. Centimeters would give a better measure.

13. Two possible answers: The width of a desk and the length of your arm. (Note: Decimeters are not commonly used in the United States.)

14. 100 bits; explanations will vary.

15. 1 cm

16. A sample class data table follows.*

Measurements to the Nearest Centimeter

Object	Measurement (nearest cm)
Height of door	223
Width of classroom	838
Length of classroom	1372
Width of board	487
Length of paper clip	3
Length of pencil	14

17. Two possible answers to measure in cm: a calculator and a computer disk. Two possible answers not to measure in cm: distance from school to home and length of side of school building.

18. A possible answer: the thickness of a pencil lead

Student Guide (p. 273)

19. $\frac{1}{1000}$

20. 10 mm = 1 cm

21. 100 mm = 1 dm. Explanations will vary.

22. A possible answer: the thickness of a dime*

Student Guide (p. 274)

23. A. 3 metersticks, 4 skinnies, 5 bits

 B. 5 skinnies, 9 bits

 C. 2 metersticks, 7 skinnies

 D. 2 metersticks, 7 bits

Next, John put down four skinnies. John said, "Each meterstick is ten decimeters, and each skinny is one decimeter long. I have two metersticks and four skinnies. So, to the nearest decimeter, this length is 24 whole decimeters."

John still had a little space left. He put down one bit. One bit is one centimeter long.

Mrs. Dewey complimented John's work: "John, you have done a terrific job. You have found the length of the board using the fewest pieces. You can write down this measurement using decimals. How many metersticks did you use?" "Two," said John.

Mrs. Dewey wrote "2." on the board. "Each decimeter is one-tenth of a meter. How many skinnies did you use?" "Four," said John.

Mrs. Dewey wrote "2.4" on the board. "Each centimeter is one-hundredth of a meter. How many bits did you use?" "One," said John.

Mrs. Dewey wrote "2.41" on the board. "This number is read two and forty-one hundredths." John showed 2.41 m with two metersticks, four skinnies, and 1 bit.

John continued to measure objects around the room to the nearest hundredth of a meter. For example, Mrs. Dewey had a life-size poster of a professional basketball player on the wall. John decided to measure the height of this player. He used 1 meterstick, 9 skinnies, and 8 bits. John wrote "1.98 meters" for this measurement. That told him the player's height was 1 meter, 9 decimeters, and 8 centimeters.

23. John wrote the following measurements on his paper. He used the fewest pieces for each measurement. How many metersticks, skinnies, and bits did John use for each measurement?
   A. 3.45 m
   B. 0.59 m
   C. 2.70 m
   D. 2.07 m

Student Guide - page 274

Student Guide (p. 275)

Homework

1. Answers will vary.

2. **A.–C.** Answers will vary.

3. Answers will vary.

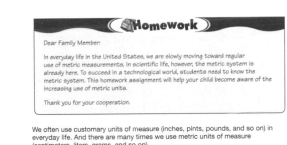

Homework

Dear Family Member:

In everyday life in the United States, we are slowly moving toward regular use of metric measurements. In scientific life, however, the metric system is already here. To succeed in a technological world, students need to know the metric system. This homework assignment will help your child become aware of the increasing use of metric units.

Thank you for your cooperation.

We often use customary units of measure (inches, pints, pounds, and so on) in everyday life. And there are many times we use metric units of measure (centimeters, liters, grams, and so on).

1. Look for metric units in the newspaper, on labels, and on other household items. Make a list showing what the unit is and what is being measured. If you can, bring in the item with the measurement on it.

2. **A.** Cut a piece of string 1 meter long.
   B. Carry your meter string with you all the time for one week.
   C. Estimate the length of various objects to the nearest meter. Then use your meter string to measure the objects to the nearest meter. Make a table showing the objects, your estimates, and your measurements.

3. Go on a measure hunt in your home. Look for objects that are between the specified lengths. Complete a data table like this one. (*Hint*: Half of your string is 0.5 m.)

Rule	Object
Between 1 and 2 m	
Between 1 and 1.5 m	
Between 0.5 and 1 m	

Student Guide - page 275

Name _____ Date _____

Unit 10 Home Practice

PART 1 *Triangle Flash Cards: 2s and 3s*
Study for the quiz on the division facts for the 2s and 3s. Take home your *Triangle Flash Cards* and your list of facts you need to study.

Here's how to use the flash cards. Ask a family member to choose one flash card at a time. He or she should cover the corner containing either the square or the circle. This number will be the answer to a division fact. Solve a division problem with the two uncovered numbers.

Your teacher will tell you when the quiz on the 2s and 3s will be. Remember to concentrate on one small group of facts each night—about 8 to 10 facts. Also, remember to study only those facts you cannot answer correctly and quickly.

PART 2 **Missing Numbers and Big Numbers**
1. What number must *n* be to make each number sentence true? After you have decided on a number for *n*, check your work by multiplying.
   A. $n \times 20 = 80$ B. $300 \times n = 1800$ C. $90 \times n = 2700$

   D. $50 \times n = 10,000$ E. $n \times 50 = 1500$ F. $70 \times n = 210$

2. A. Write the following numbers in order from smallest to largest.
   45,676   54,673   45,788   48,654   47,998   45,089

   B. Round 48,654 to the nearest thousand.

   C. Round 45,089 to the nearest hundred.

3. Use convenient numbers to estimate the answers to the following problems. Record number sentences to show your thinking.
   A. 608,965 + 28,696   B. 2,657,223 + 3,908,700   C. 378,904 − 99,645

USING DECIMALS   DAB • Grade 4 • Unit 10 **155**

Student Guide - page 155

Name _____ Date _____

Class Measurement Tables

To the Nearest Meter

Object	Measurement (nearest m)
Height of Door	
Width of Classroom	
Length of Classroom	
Width of Board	
Length of Paper Clip	
Length of Pencil	

To the Nearest Decimeter

Object	Measurement (nearest dm)
Height of Door	
Width of Classroom	
Length of Classroom	
Width of Board	
Length of Paper Clip	
Length of Pencil	

To the Nearest Centimeter

Object	Measurement (nearest cm)
Height of Door	
Width of Classroom	
Length of Classroom	
Width of Board	
Length of Paper Clip	
Length of Pencil	

m, dm, cm, mm   DAB • Grade 4 • Unit 10 • Lesson 1 **163**

Student Guide - page 163

Discovery Assignment Book (p. 155)

Home Practice*

Part 2. Missing Numbers and Big Numbers

1. A. $n = 4$ B. $n = 6$ C. $n = 30$
   D. $n = 200$ E. $n = 30$ F. $n = 3$

2. A. 45,089; 45,676; 45,788; 47,998; 48,654; 54,673
   B. 49,000   C. 45,100

3. Answers will vary. Possible answers are:
   A. $600,000 + 30,000 = 630,000$
   B. $2,700,000 + 4,000,000 = 6,700,000$
   C. $400,000 - 100,000 = 300,000$

Discovery Assignment Book (p. 163)

Class Measurement Tables[†]

See Figure 3 in the Lesson Guide and *Questions 4, 11,* and *16* in the *Student Guide* Answer Key.

---

*Answers for all the Home Practice in the *Discovery Assignment Book* are at the end of the unit.
[†]Answers and/or discussion are included in the Lesson Guide.

Discovery Assignment Book (pp. 165–166)

Measure Hunt

Answers will vary.

Measure Hunt

Find four lengths in the classroom using the rules in the table below. Use the fewest pieces possible when you measure. Use metersticks to measure meters. Use skinnies to measure decimeters. Use bits to measure centimeters. Then complete the table. An example is done for you.

Table 1

Rule	Object	Number of m	dm	cm	Length (nearest 0.01 m)
Between 1 and 2 m	Height of cabinet	1	2	0	1.20
Between 1 and 1.5 m					
Between 0.5 and 1 m					
Between 0.5 and 0.8 m					
Between 0.55 and 0.75 m					

m, dm, cm, mm   DAB • Grade 4 • Unit 10 • Lesson 1   **165**

Discovery Assignment Book - page 165

Find five lengths in the classroom using the rules in the table below. Use metersticks to measure the lengths. Then complete the table.

Table 2

Rule	Object	Number of m	dm	cm	Length (nearest 0.01 m)
Between 1 and 2 m					
Between 1 and 1.5 m					
Between 0.5 and 1 m					
Between 0.6 and 0.9 m					
Between 0.40 and 0.65 m					

166 DAB • Grade 4 • Unit 10 • Lesson 1   m, dm, cm, mm

Discovery Assignment Book - page 166

Lesson 2

Tenths

Lesson Overview

Students work with base-ten pieces to build their understanding of tenths using both common fractions and decimal fractions.

Key Content

- Translating between different representations of decimals (concrete, pictorial, verbal, and symbolic).
- Representing decimals using base-ten pieces and number charts.
- Using fractions and decimals to represent the same quantity.
- Reading and writing decimals to the tenths.

Key Vocabulary

- common fraction
- decimal fraction
- denominator
- numerator

Math Facts

DPP item G provides practice with division facts.

Homework

1. Complete the *Exploring Tenths* Activity Pages in the *Discovery Assignment Book* as homework.
2. Assign Parts 4 and 5 of the Home Practice.

Assessment

Use the *Observational Assessment Record* to document students' abilities to translate between concrete, pictorial, and symbolic representation of decimals.

Curriculum Sequence

Before This Unit

Decimals

Students explored tenths using base-ten pieces in Grade 3 Unit 15. They linked the common fraction $\frac{1}{10}$ to the decimal fraction 0.1.

After This Unit

Fractions

Students will explore common fractions in Grade 4 Unit 12.

Materials List

Supplies and Copies

Student	Teacher
Supplies for Each Student Pair • 2 packs, 14 flats, and 30 skinnies • meterstick	**Supplies** • overhead base-ten pieces
Copies	**Copies/Transparencies** • 1 transparency of *Tenths Helper* (*Discovery Assignment Book* Page 167)

All blackline masters including assessment, transparency, and DPP masters are also on the Teacher Resource CD.

Student Books
Tenths (*Student Guide* Pages 276–282)
Tenths Helper (*Discovery Assignment Book* Page 167)
Exploring Tenths (*Discovery Assignment Book* Pages 169–170)
Grace's Base-Ten Pieces (*Discovery Assignment Book* Page 171)

Daily Practice and Problems and Home Practice
DPP items E–H (*Unit Resource Guide* Pages 19–21)
Home Practice Parts 4–5 (*Discovery Assignment Book* Page 157)

Note: Classrooms whose pacing differs significantly from the suggested pacing of the units should use the Math Facts Calendar in Section 4 of the *Facts Resource Guide* to ensure students receive the complete math facts program.

Assessment Tools
Observational Assessment Record (*Unit Resource Guide* Pages 13–14)

Daily Practice and Problems

Suggestions for using the DPPs are on page 54.

E. Bit: When Does $\frac{1}{4}$ Matter? (URG p. 19)

1. Might $\frac{1}{4}$ inch be important if you are building a door?
2. Do you think $\frac{1}{4}$ inch is important when you are measuring the distance you can ride on your bike?
3. Give an example when $\frac{1}{4}$ inch is important. Give an example when it is not.

F. Task: Counting Square Units
(URG p. 19)

1. How many square millimeters are there in one square centimeter? Use the picture below to help you answer the question.

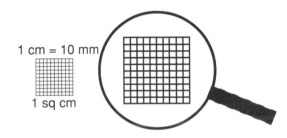

1 cm = 10 mm
1 sq cm

2. How many square centimeters are there in one square meter? It may help if you draw a picture.

G. Bit: Math Fact Practice (URG p. 20)

Solve the problem. Then write the other number sentences in the same fact family.

A. $15 \div 5 =$
B. $27 \div 3 =$
C. $16 \div 2 =$
D. $18 \div 2 =$
E. $21 \div 3 =$
F. $24 \div 3 =$
G. $2 \div 2 =$

H. Task: Addition, Subtraction, and Multiplication Practice (URG p. 21)

Use paper and pencil or mental math to solve the following problems. Be sure to estimate to see if your answers make sense.

1. A. $148 + 779 =$ B. $2090 + 793 =$
   C. $7084 - 557 =$ D. $5386 - 737 =$
   E. $94 \times 7 =$ F. $38 \times 3 =$
   G. $57 \times 2 =$ H. $4068 - 843 =$
   I. $52 \times 9 =$ J. $87 \times 3 =$

2. Explain your strategy for Question J.

Tenths

A New Rule for Base-Ten Pieces

Discuss

In the last lesson, Lee Yah used skinnies to measure to the nearest decimeter. She lined up skinnies along a meterstick. She learned that a skinny is one decimeter long and that a decimeter is one tenth of a meter.

1. **A.** How many skinnies can you lay along the edge of your meterstick?
   B. The length of one skinny is what fraction of a meterstick?

The fraction for one-tenth can be written as a common fraction ($\frac{1}{10}$). The **denominator** (the number on the bottom) tells us that the meterstick is divided into ten equal parts. The **numerator** (the number on the top) tells us that a skinny is one of these parts.

The fraction for one-tenth can also be written as a decimal fraction (0.1). The decimal point tells us that the numbers to the right of the decimal point are smaller than 1.

$$\frac{1}{10} \begin{matrix} \leftarrow \text{numerator} \\ \leftarrow \text{denominator} \end{matrix} \qquad 0.1 \begin{matrix} \\ \uparrow \\ \text{decimal point} \end{matrix}$$

2. Place 3 skinnies along the edge of the meterstick.
   A. The length of 3 skinnies is what fraction of a meter?
   B. Write this fraction as a common fraction and as a decimal fraction.

276 SG • Grade 4 • Unit 10 • Lesson 2   Tenths

Student Guide - page 276 (Answers on p. 56)

---

3. Place 5 skinnies along the edge of the meterstick.
   A. The length of 5 skinnies is what fraction of a meter?
   B. Write this fraction as a decimal fraction.
   C. Write this fraction as a common fraction in two different ways.

Doing mathematics is sometimes like playing a game. Just as you cannot play a game without rules, you cannot do mathematics without rules. But, just as people sometimes change game rules, we sometimes change rules in mathematics. And, just as we can still play a game if everyone agrees to the new rules, we can still do mathematics if everyone agrees to the new rules.

Now we are going to change a rule for base-ten pieces. When you worked with base-ten pieces before, usually a bit was one whole. When a bit is the unit, then a skinny is 10 units, a flat is 100 units, and a pack is 1000 units. Now we are going to change which piece is the whole. **For now, a flat will be one whole.**

4. Use skinnies to cover a flat.
   A. How many skinnies did you use?
   B. If a flat is 1 unit, then what fraction is a skinny?

5. **A.** Place 6 skinnies on your flat. Skip count by tenths as you place each skinny. Start like this: one-tenth, two-tenths, three-tenths....
   B. What fraction of the flat is 6 skinnies?
   C. Write this fraction as a common fraction and a decimal fraction.

Tenths   SG • Grade 4 • Unit 10 • Lesson 2 **277**

Student Guide - page 277 (Answers on p. 56)

Before the Activity

Make a transparency of the *Tenths Helper* Activity Page. Students will use base-ten pieces during the first and second parts of this lesson. During Part 1, they will use flats and skinnies. During Part 2 they will use packs, flats, and skinnies. Students will also need a meterstick and their *Tenths Helper* Activity Page during Part 1. If necessary, have students work with a partner so they can share manipulatives.

Teaching the Activity

In Part 1, measurement is used as a model for defining tenths. The base-ten pieces are then redefined for decimals. In Part 2, students continue to explore tenths using the base-ten pieces. Base-ten shorthand is used to record student work. Students explore different ways to express numbers including using the fewest pieces rule. There are several approaches to the material:

- Work through the *Tenths* Activity Pages in the *Student Guide* with students, using a teacher-led whole-class discussion. Supplement the examples in the *Student Guide* with some more of your own.

- Lead the class through activities similar to those in the *Student Guide,* using an overhead projector or board. Then assign the *Student Guide* pages to be completed individually or in small groups.

- Assign the *Tenths* Activity Pages in the *Student Guide* for students to work through with a partner or in small groups, and then discuss the pages with the whole class.

Part 1   A New Rule for Base-Ten Pieces

In *Question 1,* students are asked what fraction of the length of a meterstick is 1 skinny. Remind students of the work they did in Lesson 1 when they found that the length of 1 skinny was equal to a decimeter or $\frac{1}{10}$ of a meter. Both the common fraction and the decimal fraction for one tenth are shown. Students review the meaning of the numerator and denominator in common fractions. The meaning of the decimal point is also reviewed.

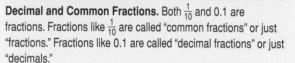

Content Note

Decimal and Common Fractions. Both $\frac{1}{10}$ and 0.1 are fractions. Fractions like $\frac{1}{10}$ are called "common fractions" or just "fractions." Fractions like 0.1 are called "decimal fractions" or just "decimals."

In *Questions 2–3,* students continue to explore decimals using skinnies and a meterstick. In *Question 3,* students place 5 skinnies along the meterstick. This represents five-tenths of a meter. Students are asked to express this fraction as a common fraction in two different ways. They should recognize that $\frac{5}{10}$ is half of the meterstick, so it can also be written $\frac{1}{2}$.

After completing these three questions, students are ready to use base-ten pieces to explore decimals. The first step in using base-ten pieces is to redefine the unit. Redefining the unit is a simple but powerful operation. In everyday life, we change our definition of the unit frequently. Depending on our point of view, we think of single eggs or eggs in dozens, of single crayons or boxes of crayons, of individual students or classes of students. Many important fraction and multiplication ideas involve changing perspectives on what "one" is.

We redefine a base-ten flat here as one whole. We could define a skinny or a pack as one whole, but they are less convenient for our purposes. Throughout the activity, the unit whole will be a flat.

With a flat as the unit, students can easily model decimals through hundredths. The *Student Guide* pages help students connect the base-ten pieces, base-ten shorthand, words, and symbols for common and decimal fractions.

In *Questions 4–7,* students explore tenths using a flat as one whole. Students skip count by tenths as they build the different numbers. Having students skip count as they place their skinnies on the flat helps them to conceptualize tenths.

Students explore the different ways to write the number 1 in *Question 7.* Review with students that $\frac{10}{10}$ means that you have divided the whole into 10 equal pieces and all ten pieces are being considered and 1.0 means that you have 1 whole and 0 tenths. Both of these are different ways of writing 1 whole.

To complete *Questions 8–11,* students will need their *Tenths Helper* Activity Page in the *Discovery Assignment Book,* as shown in Figure 4. Students use their charts to build 1 whole and 2 wholes using skinnies. Model using the chart with the overhead transparency and overhead base-ten pieces. *Question 9A* asks students to place 10 skinnies on the *Tenths Helper* Activity Page, one at a time, counting by tenths. *Question 9B* asks what number comes after nine-tenths. Be sure students understand they can say ten-tenths or

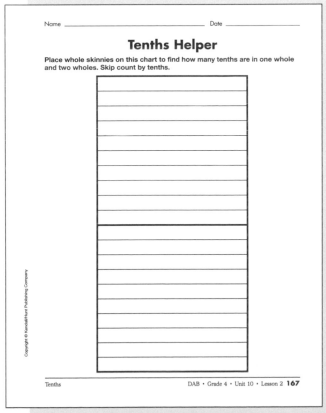

6. A. Nicholas placed 4 skinnies on his flat. Put 4 skinnies on your flat. Skip count by tenths as you place each skinny.
   B. What fraction of the flat is 4 skinnies?
   C. Write this fraction as a common fraction and a decimal fraction.

7. A. Linda placed 10 skinnies on her flat. Put 10 skinnies on your flat. Skip count by tenths as you place each skinny.
   B. How many tenths is 10 skinnies?
   C. Linda noticed that 10 skinnies covered one whole. She recorded this 3 ways: $\frac{10}{10}$, 1, and 1.0. Explain how each of these represents the same number.

You can use the *Tenths Helper* to show how many tenths are in one whole and two wholes.

8. A. Cover your *Tenths Helper* with flats. How many flats did you use?
   B. What number does this represent?

9. A. Place 10 skinnies on your *Tenths Helper*. Count by tenths as you place each skinny on the chart.
   B. When you are skip counting by tenths, what number comes after 9 tenths? (*Hint:* There is more than one answer to this question.)
   C. Continue placing skinnies on your chart. What number will you say as you place the eleventh skinny on the chart? (*Hint:* There is more than one answer to this question.)
   D. How many skinnies does it take to fill the *Tenths Helper*?
   E. How many tenths are in two wholes?

278 SG • Grade 4 • Unit 10 • Lesson 2   Tenths

Student Guide - page 278 (Answers on p. 57)

Name _____ Date _____

Tenths Helper

Place whole skinnies on this chart to find how many tenths are in one whole and two wholes. Skip count by tenths.

Tenths   DAB • Grade 4 • Unit 10 • Lesson 2 **167**

Discovery Assignment Book - page 167

Student Guide - page 279 (Answers on p. 57)

Student Guide - page 280 (Answers on p. 58)

one (whole). **Question 9C** asks students what they will say when the eleventh skinny is added. Again, students should understand they can say either "eleven-tenths" or "one and one-tenth."

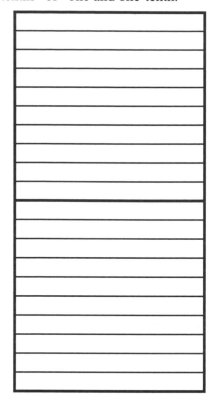

Figure 4: *A Tenths Helper chart*

Part 2 More Tenths

Use base-ten pieces on the overhead to model **Question 12.** For **Question 13,** students give the value of a pack if a flat is one whole. Help students see that a pack equals 10 by counting from one to ten as you stack 10 flats next to a pack. Base-ten shorthand is reviewed as a way to record the pieces used when building a number. See the example following **Question 13.**

Questions 14–17 can be done independently, in small groups, or together as a class. In these questions, students use base-ten pieces or base-ten shorthand to represent numbers. In **Questions 16–17,** students use base-ten shorthand to show a number between 2 and 3 and between 2.5 and 3. Give students an opportunity to share their numbers and explain why the number they chose is appropriate.

Discuss the application of the Fewest Pieces Rule. Use the base-ten pieces to show students that ten skinnies can be traded for a flat and 10 flats can be traded for a pack. Students can then complete *Questions 18–22*.

The *Exploring Tenths* and *Grace's Base-Ten Pieces* Activity Pages in the *Discovery Assignment Book* provide further exploration and practice with decimal concepts.

Journal Prompt

Compare 1.3 meters and 1.3 with base-ten blocks (A flat is one). How are 1.3 m and 1.3 flats similar? How are they different?

Content Note

Fewest Pieces Rule. While there are usually several ways to show a number using base-ten pieces, there is only one way to show a given number using the fewest base-ten pieces. Every number has a unique "fewest pieces" representation, just as every number has unique representation in our written number system.

---

16. Use base-ten pieces to make a number between 2 and 3. Use base-ten shorthand to show the pieces you used. Then write your number.

17. Use base-ten pieces to make a number between 2.5 and 3. Use base-ten shorthand to show the pieces you used. Then write your number.

The Fewest Pieces Rule

The Fewest Pieces Rule says that you should trade ten base-ten pieces for the next size up whenever you can. Ten skinnies should be traded for a flat, and ten flats should be traded for a pack. For example, you might have these base-ten pieces:

Using the Fewest Pieces Rule, you should trade ten skinnies for a flat. You would then have these pieces:

For Questions 18–20, the flat is one whole. Follow these directions:
A. Use base-ten shorthand to show how to make the number using the fewest base-ten pieces.
B. Then write a decimal for the number.

First make each number with base-ten pieces. Then trade to get the fewest pieces. Finally, write the number.

18.   ///// /////   19. ☐ ///// ///// ///// //

20. ☐ ☐ ///// ///// ///// ///

Tenths   SG • Grade 4 • Unit 10 • Lesson 2   **281**

Student Guide - page 281 (Answers on p. 58)

Name _____   Date _____

Exploring Tenths

Use base-ten shorthand to help you answer the following questions.

1. Michael placed 14 skinnies on his *Tenths Helper* chart. Write the number this represents in more than one way.

2. A. Grace wanted to build the number 1.9 on her *Tenths Helper* chart using skinnies. How many skinnies will she need to build this number?
   B. Grace decided to use both flats and skinnies to build this number. How many flats will she need? How many skinnies?

3. Nila built the following number on her *Tenths Helper* chart:

Write this number in more than one way.

4. A. Jackie placed 4 flats on her desk. How many whole units does this represent?
   B. She added 6 skinnies to the 4 flats. What number does 4 flats and 6 skinnies represent?

5. A. Jacob placed 6 skinnies along the edge of a meterstick. The length of 6 skinnies is what fraction of a meter?
   B. Write this fraction as both a decimal fraction and a common fraction.

6. A. Jessie measured the length of a table in her classroom using skinnies. She found the length of the table was 18 skinnies. How many whole meters and how many more tenths does this represent?
   B. Write the length of the table in more than one way.

Tenths   DAB • Grade 4 • Unit 10 • Lesson 2 **169**

Discovery Assignment Book - page 169 (Answers on p. 60)

Showing Numbers in Several Ways
Numbers can be shown in more than one way using base-ten pieces. Suppose a flat is one whole. Then, 2.3 can be shown in these three ways:

☐ ☐ ///
☐ ///// ///// ///
///// ///// ///// ///// ///

21. Use base-ten pieces to make 3.2 in several ways. Use base-ten shorthand to show each way you find. Circle the solution that uses the fewest pieces.

22. Work with a partner to practice making numbers with base-ten pieces. Write them, using decimals and common fractions. One person should lay out packs, flats, and skinnies. The other person should write numbers for the pieces. Keep track of your work in a table like this:

Tenths Data Table

Base-Ten Shorthand	Fraction of a Flat	
	Common	Decimal

282 SG • Grade 4 • Unit 10 • Lesson 2   Tenths

Student Guide - page 282 (Answers on p. 59)

Name _____ Date _____

7. Use what you know about tenths to complete the table by filling in the missing information. (Remember: A flat is one whole.)

Base-Ten Shorthand	Common Fraction	Decimal Fraction
////// ////	$\frac{9}{10}$	
		6.7
☐☐☐☐☐☐////		
	$23\frac{8}{10}$	
		52.3
☐☐☐☐ //// //		
☐☐☐☐☐ //		
	$34\frac{8}{10}$	
☐☐☐☐☐////		

170 DAB • Grade 4 • Unit 10 • Lesson 2   Tenths

Discovery Assignment Book - page 170 (Answers on p. 60)

Name _____ Date _____

Grace's Base-Ten Pieces

Use base-ten pieces (packs, flats, and skinnies only). A flat is one whole.

1. If a flat is 1, then what number is a pack?

2. If a flat is 1, then what number is a skinny?

Grace has two base-ten pieces. She might have skinnies, flats, or packs. For example, she might have a skinny and a flat. She might have something else.

3. Find all possible sets of pieces that Grace might have. Use base-ten shorthand to show each set she might have. Write a number for each set.

4. What is the largest number that Grace could possibly have?

5. What is the smallest number that Grace could possibly have?

6. Put the numbers that Grace could have in order from smallest to largest.

Tenths   DAB • Grade 4 • Unit 10 • Lesson 2 **171**

Discovery Assignment Book - page 171 (Answers on p. 61)

Math Facts

DPP item G provides practice with fact families.

Homework and Practice

- Assign the *Exploring Tenths* Activity Pages in the *Discovery Assignment Book* for homework.
- DPP items E and F provide practice with measurement. Item H provides computation practice.
- Assign Parts 4 and 5 of the Home Practice.

Answers for Parts 4 and 5 of the Home Practice are in the Answer Key at the end of this lesson and at the end of this unit.

Assessment

- You can use *Grace's Base-Ten Pieces* as a pre-assessment activity to get your students ready for the assessment activity in Lesson 3.
- Use Homework *Question 7* on the *Exploring Tenths* Activity Pages in the *Discovery Assignment Book* to assess your students' abilities to translate between symbols and physical models for decimals.
- Use the Assessment Indicators as you observe your students working with the base-ten pieces. Use the *Observational Assessment Record* to record students' abilities to translate between concrete, pictorial, and symbolic representations of decimals.

Name _____ Date _____

PART 4 School Supplies

Linda and her brother are buying school supplies. Notebooks are on sale for 39¢ each. Pencils are 4 for $1.00. A set of markers costs $2.98. Folders are 10 for $1.00.

1. Linda needs 3 notebooks, 1 set of markers, 1 folder, and 8 pencils. Estimate the cost of Linda's school supplies. Write number sentences to show your thinking.

2. Linda's brother needs 5 notebooks, 1 set of markers, 3 folders, and 4 pencils. Estimate the cost of his school supplies. Write number sentences to show your thinking.

3. What is the exact cost of each child's supplies? (There is no tax.)

4. What is the difference in price between the two children's supplies? Write a number sentence to show how you solved the problem.

PART 5 Addition, Subtraction, and Multiplication

Solve the following problems using paper and pencil or mental math. Estimate to make sure your answers are reasonable.

1. A. 68 − 49 =   B. 167 + 67 =   C. 284 + 238 =   D. 432 − 197 =

   E. 47 × 9 =   F. 26 × 7 =   G. 34 × 9 =   H. 23 × 8 =

2. Explain your estimation strategy for Question 1F.

3. Explain a possible mental math strategy for Question 1D.

USING DECIMALS   DAB • Grade 4 • Unit 10 **157**

Discovery Assignment Book - page 157 (Answers on p. 59)

At a Glance

Math Facts and Daily Practice and Problems

DPP items E and F provide practice with measurement. Bit G provides practice with division facts. Task H provides computation practice.

Part 1. A New Rule for Base-Ten Pieces

1. Lay skinnies along the edge of a meterstick to see that the length of one skinny is one-tenth the length of a meterstick.
2. Write one-tenth as a common fraction. Review the information the numerator and denominator provide. *(Questions 1–3)*
3. Write one-tenth as a decimal fraction. Review the function of the decimal point.
4. Redefine the base-ten pieces. One flat equals one whole.
5. Use skinnies and flats to represent various decimal numbers. *(Questions 4–7)*
6. Use *Questions 8–9* in the *Student Guide* and the *Tenths Helper* Activity Page in the *Discovery Assignment Book* to show how many tenths are in one whole and in two wholes.
7. Students use skinnies to show numbers on the *Tenths Helper* Activity Page. They then write the numbers using common fractions and decimals. *(Questions 10–11)*

Part 2. More Tenths

1. If the flat is one whole, show that the value of a pack is 10. *(Questions 12–13)*
2. Use base-ten shorthand to record the pieces you use to make a number. *(Question 14)*
3. Write a decimal and a common fraction for base-ten shorthand. *(Questions 15–17)*
4. Represent numbers using the fewest pieces rule. *(Questions 18–20)*
5. Represent numbers in more than one way using base-ten pieces. *(Questions 21–22)*
6. Complete *Grace's Base-Ten Pieces* as a pre-assessment activity.

Homework

1. Complete the *Exploring Tenths* Activity Pages in the *Discovery Assignment Book* as homework.
2. Assign Parts 4 and 5 of the Home Practice for homework.

Assessment

Use the *Observational Assessment Record* to document students' abilities to translate between concrete, pictorial, and symbolic representation of decimals.

Answer Key is on pages 56–61.

Notes:

Student Guide - page 276

Student Guide - page 277

Student Guide (p. 276)

Tenths

1.* **A.** 10 skinnies

   B. $\frac{1}{10}$ or 0.1 m

2. **A.** three-tenths meter

   B. $\frac{3}{10}$ and 0.3

Student Guide (p. 277)

3. **A.** five-tenths meter

   B. 0.5

   C. $\frac{5}{10}$ m $= \frac{1}{2}$ m*

4. **A.** 10 skinnies

   B. $\frac{1}{10}$

5. **B.** six-tenths

   C. $\frac{6}{10}$ and 0.6

*Answers and/or discussion are included in the Lesson Guide.

Student Guide (p. 278)

6. B. four-tenths

C. $\frac{4}{10}$ and 0.4

7. B. 10 tenths

C. The ten in the denominator of $\frac{10}{10}$ means that the whole is divided into 10 equal parts and the 10 in the numerator means we are interested in all ten parts. 1 means one whole and 1.0 represents 1 whole and no tenths. All three represent the same number.*

8. A. 2 flats

B. 2

9. B. ten-tenths or one whole*

C. eleven-tenths or one and one-tenth*

D. 20 skinnies

E. 20 tenths

Student Guide (p. 279)

10. A. $\frac{17}{10}$, $1\frac{7}{10}$, or 1.7

B. $\frac{4}{10}$ or 0.4 (Just writing .4 is acceptable.)

C. $\frac{15}{10}$, $1\frac{5}{10}$, or 1.5

D. $\frac{9}{10}$ or 0.9

E. $\frac{1}{10}$ or 0.1

F. $\frac{13}{10}$, $1\frac{3}{10}$, or 1.3

G. $\frac{18}{10}$, $1\frac{8}{10}$, 1.8

11.

Decimal	Mixed	Fraction
0.1		$\frac{1}{10}$
0.2		$\frac{2}{10}$
0.3		$\frac{3}{10}$
0.4		$\frac{4}{10}$
0.5		$\frac{5}{10}$
0.6		$\frac{6}{10}$
0.7		$\frac{7}{10}$
0.8		$\frac{8}{10}$
0.9		$\frac{9}{10}$
1.0		$\frac{10}{10}$
1.1	$1\frac{1}{10}$	$\frac{11}{10}$
1.2	$1\frac{2}{10}$	$\frac{12}{10}$
1.3	$1\frac{3}{10}$	$\frac{13}{10}$
1.4	$1\frac{4}{10}$	$\frac{14}{10}$
1.5	$1\frac{5}{10}$	$\frac{15}{10}$
1.6	$1\frac{6}{10}$	$\frac{16}{10}$
1.7	$1\frac{7}{10}$	$\frac{17}{10}$
1.8	$1\frac{8}{10}$	$\frac{18}{10}$
1.9	$1\frac{9}{10}$	$\frac{19}{10}$
2.0	$1\frac{10}{10}$	$\frac{20}{10}$

6. A. Nicholas placed 4 skinnies on his flat. Put 4 skinnies on your flat. Skip count by tenths as you place each skinny.
   B. What fraction of the flat is 4 skinnies?
   C. Write this fraction as a common fraction and a decimal fraction.

7. A. Linda placed 10 skinnies on her flat. Put 10 skinnies on your flat. Skip count by tenths as you place each skinny.
   B. How many tenths is 10 skinnies?
   C. Linda noticed that 10 skinnies covered one whole. She recorded this 3 ways: $\frac{10}{10}$, 1, and 1.0. Explain how each of these represents the same number.

You can use the *Tenths Helper* to show how many tenths are in one whole and two wholes.

8. A. Cover your *Tenths Helper* with flats. How many flats did you use?
   B. What number does this represent?

9. A. Place 10 skinnies on your *Tenths Helper*. Count by tenths as you place each skinny on the chart.
   B. When you are skip counting by tenths, what number comes after 9 tenths? (*Hint:* There is more than one answer to this question.)
   C. Continue placing skinnies on your chart. What number will you say as you place the eleventh skinny on the chart? (*Hint:* There is more than one answer to this question.)
   D. How many skinnies does it take to fill the *Tenths Helper*?
   E. How many tenths are in two wholes?

278 SG • Grade 4 • Unit 10 • Lesson 2   Tenths

Student Guide - page 278

Explore

Keenya uses a *Tenths Helper* to show tenths. First she places 12 skinnies on the chart. She counts by tenths as she places each skinny. Then she records the value of 12 skinnies on the chart.

Place 12 skinnies on your chart.   Then record the value in more than one way.

Use the *Tenths Helper* to complete Questions 10–11. Use the skinnies to show each number. Then record its value on the chart in more than one way.

10. A. 17 skinnies
    B. 4 skinnies
    C. 15 skinnies
    D. 9 skinnies
    E. 1 skinny
    F. 13 skinnies
    G. 18 skinnies

11. Fill in all of the values in your *Tenths Helper*. If needed, use skinnies to build each number.

Tenths   SG • Grade 4 • Unit 10 • Lesson 2 279

Student Guide - page 279

*Answers and/or discussion are included in the Lesson Guide.

Student Guide - page 280

Student Guide - page 281

Student Guide (p. 280)

12. 4.6

13. 10*

14. A. □ /|\| /|

  B. □□□ /|\|

  C. |\|/| /

  D. □ □□□ /|

  E. □ |

15. A. $2\frac{5}{10}$ and 2.5

  B. $12\frac{4}{10}$ and 12.4

  C. $\frac{9}{10}$ and 0.9

  D. 10.3 and $10\frac{3}{10}$

Student Guide (p. 281)

16. Answers will vary

17. Answers will vary.

18. A. □

  B. 1 or 1.0

19. A. □ □ |\|/| ||

  B. 11.7

20. A. □□□ |\|/| /||

  B. 3.8

*Answers and/or discussion are included in the Lesson Guide.

Student Guide (p. 282)

21. Answers will vary.

22. Answers will vary.

Showing Numbers in Several Ways
Numbers can be shown in more than one way using base-ten pieces. Suppose a flat is one whole. Then, 2.3 can be shown in these three ways:

21. Use base-ten pieces to make 3.2 in several ways. Use base-ten shorthand to show each way you find. Circle the solution that uses the fewest pieces.

22. Work with a partner to practice making numbers with base-ten pieces. Write them, using decimals and common fractions. One person should lay out packs, flats, and skinnies. The other person should write numbers for the pieces. Keep track of your work in a table like this:

Tenths Data Table

| Base-Ten Shorthand | Fraction of a Flat | |
	Common	Decimal

282 SG • Grade 4 • Unit 10 • Lesson 2   Tenths

Student Guide - page 282

Discovery Assignment Book (p. 157)

Home Practice*

Part 4. School Supplies

1. $3 \times \$0.40 = \$1.20$;
   $\$1.20 + \$3 + \$0.10 + \$2 = \$6.30$

2. $5 \times \$0.40 = \$2$;
   $\$2 + \$3 + \$0.30 + \$1 = \$6.30$

3. Linda: $6.25
   Linda's brother: $6.23

4. $\$6.25 - \$6.23 = \$0.02$ or 2¢

Part 5. Addition, Subtraction, and Multiplication

1. **A.** 19   **B.** 234
   C. 522   **D.** 235
   E. 423   **F.** 182
   G. 306   **H.** 184

2. Possible strategy: 26×7 is close to 25×7. Skip count by 25s seven times: 25, 50, 75, 100, 125, 150, 175. 26×7 is about 175.

3. Possible strategy: $432 - 197$ is the same as $435 - 200 = 235$.

Name _____ Date _____

PART 4 School Supplies
Linda and her brother are buying school supplies. Notebooks are on sale for 39¢ each. Pencils are 4 for $1.00. A set of markers costs $2.98. Folders are 10 for $1.00.

1. Linda needs 3 notebooks, 1 set of markers, 1 folder, and 8 pencils. Estimate the cost of Linda's school supplies. Write number sentences to show your thinking.

2. Linda's brother needs 5 notebooks, 1 set of markers, 3 folders, and 4 pencils. Estimate the cost of his school supplies. Write number sentences to show your thinking.

3. What is the exact cost of each child's supplies? (There is no tax.)

4. What is the difference in price between the two children's supplies? Write a number sentence to show how you solved the problem.

PART 5 Addition, Subtraction, and Multiplication
Solve the following problems using paper and pencil or mental math. Estimate to make sure your answers are reasonable.

1. A. 68 − 49 =   B. 167 + 67 =   C. 284 + 238 =   D. 432 − 197 =
   E. 47 × 9 =   F. 26 × 7 =   G. 34 × 9 =   H. 23 × 8 =

2. Explain your estimation strategy for Question 1F.

3. Explain a possible mental math strategy for Question 1D.

USING DECIMALS   DAB • Grade 4 • Unit 10 **157**

Discovery Assignment Book - page 157

*Answers for all the Home Practice in the *Discovery Assignment Book* are at the end of the unit.

Name _____ Date _____

Exploring Tenths

Use base-ten shorthand to help you answer the following questions.

1. Michael placed 14 skinnies on his *Tenths Helper* chart. Write the number this represents in more than one way.

2. **A.** Grace wanted to build the number 1.9 on her *Tenths Helper* chart using skinnies. How many skinnies will she need to build this number?

   B. Grace decided to use both flats and skinnies to build this number. How many flats will she need? How many skinnies?

3. Nila built the following number on her *Tenths Helper* chart:

   Write this number in more than one way.

4. **A.** Jackie placed 4 flats on her desk. How many whole units does this represent?

   B. She added 6 skinnies to the 4 flats. What number does 4 flats and 6 skinnies represent?

5. **A.** Jacob placed 6 skinnies along the edge of a meterstick. The length of 6 skinnies is what fraction of a meter?

   B. Write this fraction as both a decimal fraction and a common fraction.

6. **A.** Jessie measured the length of a table in her classroom using skinnies. She found the length of the table was 18 skinnies. How many whole meters and how many more tenths does this represent?

   B. Write the length of the table in more than one way.

Tenths   DAB • Grade 4 • Unit 10 • Lesson 2 **169**

Discovery Assignment Book - page 169

Discovery Assignment Book (p. 169)

Exploring Tenths

1. $\frac{14}{10}$, $1\frac{4}{10}$, and 1.4

2. **A.** 19 skinnies

   B. 1 flat and 9 skinnies

3. $\frac{7}{10}$ and 0.7

4. **A.** 4 wholes

   B. 4.6

5. **A.** 0.6 m

   B. $\frac{6}{10}$ or 0.6

6. 1 whole meter and 8 tenths (1.8 m)

Name _____ Date _____

7. Use what you know about tenths to complete the table by filling in the missing information. (Remember: A flat is one whole.)

Base-Ten Shorthand	Common Fraction	Decimal Fraction
||||| |||||	$\frac{9}{10}$	
		6.7
⬜⬜⬜⬜⬜///		
	$23\frac{8}{10}$	
		52.3
⬜⬜⬜⬜//// //		
⬜⬜⬜⬜⬜ //		
	$34\frac{5}{10}$	
⬜⬜⬜⬜⬜////		

170 DAB • Grade 4 • Unit 10 • Lesson 2   Tenths

Discovery Assignment Book - page 170

Discovery Assignment Book (p. 170)

7.

Base-Ten Shorthand	Common Fraction	Decimal Fraction
||||| |||||	$\frac{9}{10}$	0.9
⬜⬜⬜⬜⬜ |//||	$6\frac{7}{10}$	6.7
⬜⬜⬜⬜⬜ ///	$33\frac{4}{10}$	33.4
⬜⬜ ⬜⬜⬜ |//| /	$23\frac{6}{10}$	23.6
⬜⬜⬜⬜⬜⬜ //	$52\frac{3}{10}$	52.3
⬜⬜⬜⬜ ||||| //	$40\frac{7}{10}$	40.7
⬜⬜⬜⬜⬜ /	$5\frac{2}{10}$	5.2
⬜⬜⬜⬜⬜⬜ /|||	$34\frac{5}{10}$	34.5
⬜⬜⬜⬜⬜////	$15\frac{4}{10}$	15.4

Discovery Assignment Book (p. 171)

Grace's Base-Ten Pieces

1. 10
2. 0.1
3. 20

    11

    10.1

    2

    1.1

    0.2

4. 20
5. 0.2
6. 0.2, 1.1, 2, 10.1, 11, 20

Name _____ Date _____

Grace's Base-Ten Pieces

Use base-ten pieces (packs, flats, and skinnies only). A flat is one whole.

1. If a flat is 1, then what number is a pack?

2. If a flat is 1, then what number is a skinny?

Grace has two base-ten pieces. She might have skinnies, flats, or packs. For example, she might have a skinny and a flat. She might have something else.

3. Find all possible sets of pieces that Grace might have. Use base-ten shorthand to show each set she might have. Write a number for each set.

4. What is the largest number that Grace could possibly have?

5. What is the smallest number that Grace could possibly have?

6. Put the numbers that Grace could have in order from smallest to largest.

Tenths   DAB • Grade 4 • Unit 10 • Lesson 2 **171**

Discovery Assignment Book - page 171

Lesson 3

Hundredths

Lesson Overview

Estimated Class Sessions

3

Students work with base-ten pieces to build their understanding of decimals through hundredths using both common fractions and decimal fractions. An assessment activity concludes the lesson.

Key Content

- Translating between different representations of decimals (concrete, pictorial, verbal, and symbolic).
- Representing decimals using base-ten pieces and number charts.
- Using fractions and decimals to represent the same quantity.
- Reading and writing decimals to the hundredths' place.

Key Vocabulary

- denominator
- hundredth
- numerator

Math Facts

DPP Bits K and M provide math facts practice.

Homework

1. Assign the *More Hundredths* Activity Pages in the *Discovery Assignment Book* after Part 1.
2. Assign the Homework section, *Playing Hundredths, Hundredths, Hundredths,* in the *Student Guide* after Part 2.
3. Assign Home Practice Part 3.

Assessment

1. Score the *Linda's Base-Ten Pieces* Assessment Blackline Master using the Knowing dimension of the *TIMS Multidimensional Rubric.*
2. Use the *Observational Assessment Record* to document students' abilities to translate between different representations of decimals.

Materials List

Supplies and Copies

Student	Teacher
Supplies for Each Student Pair • 2 packs, 14 flats, 30 skinnies, and 50 bits	**Supplies** • overhead base-ten pieces, optional
Copies • 1 copy of *Linda's Base-Ten Pieces* per student (*Unit Resource Guide* Page 73)	**Copies/Transparencies** • 1 transparency of *Shorthand and Fractions Table* (*Discovery Assignment Book* Page 177) • 1 copy of *TIMS Multidimensional Rubric,* optional (*Teacher Implementation Guide,* Assessment section) • 1 transparency or poster of Student Rubric: *Knowing* (*Teacher Implementation Guide,* Assessment section)

All blackline masters including assessment, transparency, and DPP masters are also on the Teacher Resource CD.

Student Books
Hundredths (*Student Guide* Pages 283–287)
Student Rubric: *Knowing* (*Student Guide* Appendix A and Inside Back Cover)
More Hundredths (*Discovery Assignment Book* Pages 173–174)
Hundredths, Hundredths, Hundredths (*Discovery Assignment Book* Page 175)
Shorthand and Fractions Table (*Discovery Assignment Book* Page 177)

Daily Practice and Problems and Home Practice
DPP items I–N (*Unit Resource Guide* Pages 21–24)
Home Practice Part 3 (*Discovery Assignment Book* Page 156)

Note: Classrooms whose pacing differs significantly from the suggested pacing of the units should use the Math Facts Calendar in Section 4 of the *Facts Resource Guide* to ensure students receive the complete math facts program.

Assessment Tools
Observational Assessment Record (*Unit Resource Guide* Pages 13–14)
TIMS Multidimensional Rubric (*Teacher Implementation Guide,* Assessment section), optional

Daily Practice and Problems

Suggestions for using the DPPs are on page 70.

I. Bit: Number Line Decimals

(URG p. 21)

The picture below shows a piece of a centimeter ruler enlarged. For each letter, write the decimal that matches.

J. Task: Line Symmetry (URG p. 22)

Parts of the pictures below are missing. The dashed lines are lines of symmetry. Copy or trace the pictures on paper and draw in the missing parts.

K. Bit: The Price Is Right (URG p. 22)

Fill in the table. Find the largest second factor so that the product of the two numbers is close to the target number without going over the target number. The first has been filled in for you.

Factor 1	Factor 2	Target Number	Left Over
5	7	38	3
3		28	
2		17	
7		25	
6		20	
9		48	
4		13	
5		12	

L. Task: Measuring Angles

(URG p. 23)

You will need a ruler and a protractor to do these problems.

1. Draw a triangle. Make one angle 38°.
2. Draw a quadrilateral. Make one angle 125°.
3. Draw a hexagon. Make one angle 70°.

M. Bit: Multiplying with Zeros

(URG p. 23)

A. $80 \times 20 =$ B. $40 \times 3 =$

C. $3000 \times 40 =$ D. $20 \times 500 =$

E. $50 \times 30 =$ F. $600 \times 2 =$

G. $0 \times 20 =$ H. $10 \times 60 =$

N. Challenge: Time (URG p. 24)

1 day = 24 hours

1 hour = 60 minutes

1 minute = 60 seconds

1 week = 7 days

1. 5 hours = ? minutes
2. 4 weeks = ? days
3. 3 days = ? hours
4. $\frac{1}{2}$ hour = ? minutes
5. $\frac{1}{4}$ day = ? hours
6. $\frac{1}{10}$ minute = ? seconds
7. 360 minutes = ? hours
8. 42 days = ? weeks

You will need a transparency of the *Shorthand and Fractions Table* Activity Page in the *Discovery Assignment Book.* This can be used to introduce the game *Hundredths, Hundredths, Hundredths.* It can also provide additional practice for students as needed. Students will use base-ten pieces—packs, flats, skinnies, and bits. You may want students to work with a partner so they can share manipulatives.

Teaching the Activity

There are three parts to this lesson. In the first part, students explore hundredths using a variety of contexts. Students write base-ten shorthand to record the base-ten pieces used to show numbers. You can use one of the following approaches to Part 1:

• Work through the *Hundredths* Activity Pages in the *Student Guide* in a teacher-led whole-class discussion. Supplement the examples in the *Student Guide* with some more of your own.

• Lead the class through activities similar to those in the *Student Guide,* using an overhead projector or board. Then, assign the activity pages to be completed with a partner or in small groups.

In the second part of this lesson, students play a game, *Hundredths, Hundredths, Hundredths.* In Part 3, they complete the *Linda's Base-Ten Pieces* Assessment Blackline Master. Score this assessment using the Knowing dimension of the *TIMS Multidimensional Rubric.*

Part 1 Exploring Hundredths

This lesson begins with a short vignette in the *Student Guide.* Jackie recognizes that since there are 100 pennies in one dollar, a penny is $\frac{1}{100}$ of a dollar. This can be written as a common fraction ($\frac{1}{100}$) or as a decimal fraction (0.01). In *Question 1,* students are asked what information the **denominator** and the **numerator** give us in a common fraction. Review with students that the denominator tells us how many equal pieces the whole is divided into. In the case of $\frac{1}{100}$, the whole is divided into 100 equal pieces. The numerator tells us how many of the equal parts we are considering. In the case of $\frac{1}{100}$, we are considering one of the equal parts. A penny is one-hundredth of a dollar. Students are then asked to tell what the zeros mean in the decimal fraction 0.01. The zero to the left of the decimal point tells us there are no whole values. The zero to the right of the decimal point tells us there are no tenths.

In *Question 2,* students find out what fraction of a dollar 14 pennies represent. They express their answers both as common fractions and as decimal fractions.

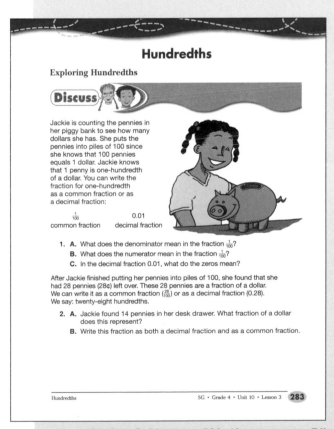

Student Guide - page 283 (Answers on p. 74)

Student Guide - page 284 *(Answers on p. 74)*

Student Guide - page 285 *(Answers on p. 75)*

In Lesson 1, students learned that since there are 100 centimeters in 1 meter, 1 centimeter is equal to $\frac{1}{100}$ of a meter. In *Question 3,* students are asked what fraction of a meter is 15 centimeters. If students have difficulty answering this question, show them on a meterstick what 15 cm looks like.

Students then extend their understanding of decimals to the base-ten pieces. In Lesson 2, a flat was defined as one, a pack as ten, and a skinny as one-tenth. Students are asked to suggest a piece that will show one-hundredth in *Question 4.* They should suggest a bit. If they don't, prompt them by placing a flat on the overhead reminding students that a flat is one whole. Ask:

- *What base-ten piece would we use if we wanted to divide the flat into 10 equal parts?* (A skinny is one-tenth of a flat.)
- *What piece would we use if we wanted to divide the flat into 100 equal parts?* (A bit is one-hundredth of a flat.)

In *Question 5A,* students are asked how many hundredths a skinny represents. Make sure students understand that a skinny is ten-hundredths. Show them that this can be written as 0.10 or 0.1. It can also be expressed as the common fractions $\frac{1}{10}$ or $\frac{10}{100}$. Help students see that these are all equal by laying 10 bits or ten-hundredths along the side of one skinny or one-tenth. In *Question 5B,* students are also asked how many hundredths a flat represents. Show students that this can be written as $\frac{100}{100}$, as 1, or as 1.00.

In *Questions 6–8,* numbers are represented with base-ten pieces. Students are to give the common fraction and the decimal fraction for each number. In *Question 6,* students are shown the base-ten pieces representing 2.03, as shown in Figure 5. Make sure students understand that these base-ten pieces represent 2 wholes, zero tenths, and three-hundredths. Provide similar examples for more practice.

Figure 5: *Base-ten pieces showing 2.03*

Question 9 reviews the use of base-ten shorthand to record the pieces used to show each number.

Questions 9–16 provide additional practice. Students may work on these with a partner or in small groups. Solutions can then be shared in class as time permits.

Assign the *More Hundredths* Activity Pages in the *Discovery Assignment Book* as homework.

Part 2 *Hundredths, Hundredths, Hundredths*

This game is in the *Discovery Assignment Book.*
Each pair of students will need flats, skinnies,
and bits to play the game, as well as a copy of the
Shorthand and Fractions Table Activity Page in the
Discovery Assignment Book. Introduce the game
using an overhead transparency of the *Shorthand
and Fractions Table* Activity Page. Ask two students
to demonstrate the game or play a sample game
with a student. Begin by reviewing the rules on the
Hundredths, Hundredths, Hundredths Activity Page.
The first player builds a number using base-ten
pieces and records his or her number using base-ten
shorthand. The second player then records both the
common fraction and the decimal fraction for the
number and says the number out loud. If the second
player does all three things correctly, he or she
receives 3 points. If any part of the second player's
response is incorrect, he or she will lose a point for
the incorrect part. For example, if the player says
the number correctly, writes the common fraction
correctly, but writes the decimal fraction incorrectly,
he or she would earn 2 points. Play several rounds
during the demonstration game. Be sure to include
some examples of numbers that are made without
following the fewest pieces rule such as the example
at the bottom of the game page, which shows 2.41.
Allow time for students to play the game in class.

11. **A.** Use base-ten pieces to make 0.1 and 0.2.
    B. Use base-ten pieces to make a number more than 0.1 but less than 0.2. Use base-ten shorthand to show the pieces you used. Then write your number.

12. **A.** Use base-ten pieces to make 2.5 and 2.6.
    B. Use base-ten pieces to make a number more than 2.5 but less than 2.6. Use base-ten shorthand to show the pieces you used. Then write your number.

For Questions 13–15, use base-ten shorthand to show how to make the number using the fewest base-ten pieces. Then write a decimal for the number.

13.

14.

15.

16. If you do not follow the fewest base-ten pieces rule, then the same number can be shown in several ways. Use base-ten pieces to make 0.42 in several ways. Use base-ten shorthand to show each way you find.

Homework

Playing *Hundredths, Hundredths, Hundredths*

Complete these questions after playing *Hundredths, Hundredths, Hundredths.*

1. Lee Yah and Jerome were playing *Hundredths, Hundredths, Hundredths.* Jerome tried to trick Lee Yah by making this number:

Student Guide - page 286 (Answers on p. 76)

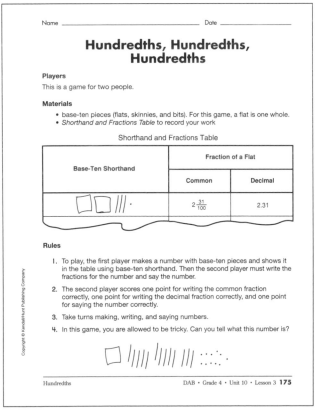

Name _____ Date _____

Hundredths, Hundredths, Hundredths

Players
This is a game for two people.

Materials
• base-ten pieces (flats, skinnies, and bits). For this game, a flat is one whole.
• *Shorthand and Fractions Table* to record your work

Shorthand and Fractions Table

Base-Ten Shorthand	Fraction of a Flat	
	Common	Decimal
	$2\frac{31}{100}$	2.31

Rules

1. To play, the first player makes a number with base-ten pieces and shows it in the table using base-ten shorthand. Then the second player must write the fractions for the number and say the number.

2. The second player scores one point for writing the common fraction correctly, one point for writing the decimal fraction correctly, and one point for saying the number correctly.

3. Take turns making, writing, and saying numbers.

4. In this game, you are allowed to be tricky. Can you tell what this number is?

Discovery Assignment Book - page 175

Name _____ Date _____

Shorthand and Fractions Table

You need base-ten pieces. For this page, a flat is one whole.

Base-Ten Shorthand	Fraction of a Flat	
	Common	Decimal

Discovery Assignment Book - page 177

The *Linda's Base-Ten Pieces* Assessment Blackline Master assesses students' understanding of decimal notation through hundredths. This activity parallels the *Grace's Base-Ten Pieces* pre-assessment page completed in Lesson 2. In this activity, however, students use packs, flats, skinnies, and bits. Score the assessment using the Knowing dimension of the *TIMS Multidimensional Rubric*. Review the Student Rubric: *Knowing* before beginning the assessment to remind students of your expectations. The following student work has been scored using the Knowing dimension.

Written Work from Student A

Linda's Base-Ten Pieces

You need base-ten pieces (packs, flats, skinnies, and bits.) A flat is one whole.

1. If a flat is 1, then what number is a pack?   10

2. If a flat is 1, then what number is a skinny?   1/10

3. If a flat is 1, then what number is a bit?   1/100

Linda has two base-ten pieces. She might have bits, skinnies, flats, or packs. For example, she might have two flats. She might have something else.

4. Find all the possible sets of pieces that Linda might have. Use base-ten shorthand to show each set she might have. Write the number for each set.

5. What is the largest number that Linda could possibly have?

6. What is the smallest number that Linda could possibly have?

7. Put the numbers that Linda could have in order from smallest to largest.

Knowing	Level 4	Level 3	Level 2	Level 1
Understands the task's mathematical concepts, their properties and applications...	Completely	Nearly completely	Partially	Not at all
Translates between words, pictures, symbols, tables, graphs, and real situations...	Readily and without errors	With minor errors	With major errors	Not at all
Uses tools (measuring devices, graphs, tables, calculators, etc.) and procedures...	Correctly and efficiently	Correctly or with minor errors	Incorrectly	Not at all
Uses knowledge of the facts of mathematics (geometry definitions, math facts, etc.)...	Correctly	With minor errors	With major errors	Not at all

Student A scored at a level 2 for this task. She correctly identified the value of the pack, skinny, and bit and was able to show 3 possible sets of pieces Linda might have. She did not, however, write a number for any of the three sets. This incomplete answer does not show whether the student has full understanding of the math called for in the problem. The student answered *Questions 5–7* correctly based on her answer to *Question 4,* but, these answers are incomplete. This student used symbols to answer *Questions 5–7* instead of using the common fraction or the decimal fraction. By doing so, she does not show that she understands how to translate between the pictorial and the symbolic representations.

Written Work from Student B

Linda's Base-Ten Pieces

You need base-ten pieces (packs, flats, skinnies, and bits.) A flat is one whole.

1. If a flat is 1, then what number is a pack?   *10*

2. If a flat is 1, then what number is a skinny?   *.1*

3. If a flat is 1, then what number is a bit?   *.01*

Linda has two base-ten pieces. She might have bits, skinnies, flats, or packs. For example, she might have two flats. She might have something else.

4. *Find all the possible sets of pieces that Linda might have. Use base-ten shorthand to show each set she might have. Write the number for each set.* *(student handwritten base-ten shorthand figures)*

02, 2 2 20, .11, 10, 10.0, 11, .1, 10.1

5. What is the largest number that Linda could possibly have?
    20

6. What is the smallest number that Linda could possibly have?
    .02

7. Put the numbers that Linda could have in order from smallest to largest.
    .02 .12 ... 1.1, .2, 10.01, 10,1, 11, 20

Knowing	Level 4	Level 3	Level 2	Level 1
Understands the task's mathematical concepts, their properties and applications…	Completely (X)	Nearly completely	Partially	Not at all
Translates between words, pictures, symbols, tables, graphs, and real situations…	Readily and without errors	With minor errors (X)	With major errors	Not at all
Uses tools (measuring devices, graphs, tables, calculators, etc.) and procedures…	Correctly and efficiently (X)	Correctly or with minor errors	Incorrectly	Not at all
Uses knowledge of the facts of mathematics (geometry definitions, math facts, etc.)…	Correctly (X)	With minor errors	With major errors	Not at all

Student B scored at level 4 for this task. It is evident that this student clearly understood each step of this task and how these steps were related to each other. He added the number .21 in *Question 7.* This indicated a minor error translating between the pictures in *Question 4* and the ordering of numbers in *Question 7.* This student found all the possible sets of pieces that Linda could have. He organized his work by first listing in base-ten shorthand all the possible doubles. He then listed all the other possibilities systematically. This organization enabled him to make sure he had all the possible solutions.

Discovery Assignment Book - page 173

Name _____ Date _____

More Hundredths

Making a Hundredths Chart

Professor Peabody made a hundredths chart. He forgot to fill in some of the chart. Help Professor Peabody by filling in the missing values.

0.01	0.02				0.06				0.1
	0.12			0.15			0.18		
0.21			0.24			0.27			
0.31		0.33			0.36				0.4
				0.45			0.48		
	0.52								
0.61				0.65				0.69	0.7
		0.73			0.76			0.79	
0.81							0.88		0.9
0.91		0.93				0.97			1

Use your completed chart to answer the following questions.

1. A. What number comes after 0.09?

   B. Why is it recorded as 0.1?

2. What number comes after 0.99?

3. Describe any patterns that you see in your hundredths chart.

Hundredths   DAB • Grade 4 • Unit 10 • Lesson 3 **173**

Discovery Assignment Book - page 173 (Answers on p. 78)

Name _____ Date _____

4. Use base-ten shorthand to make these numbers.

   A. 19.06

   B. 0.68

   C. 1.73

   D. 44.4

5. Give a decimal fraction and a common fraction for the base-ten shorthand below:

   A.

   B.

   C.

   D.

   E.

174 DAB • Grade 4 • Unit 10 • Lesson 3   Hundredths

Discovery Assignment Book - page 174 (Answers on p. 78)

Math Facts

DPP Bit K provides practice with division facts by solving problems in which the division does not come out evenly. DPP Bit M provides practice multiplying with multiples of 10.

Homework and Practice

- *More Hundredths* Activity Pages in the *Discovery Assignment Book* can be assigned after Part 1 of this lesson.

- *Questions 1–7* in the Homework section in the *Student Guide* can be assigned after Part 2 of this lesson.

- For more practice, make up a worksheet using the *Shorthand and Fractions Table.*

- DPP Bit I provides practice reading centimeters to the nearest tenth on a ruler. Tasks J and L are exercises in geometry. J involves symmetry and L involves drawing figures correctly. DPP Challenge N provides practice converting between different units of time.

- Home Practice Part 3 can be assigned as homework for extra practice.

Answers for Part 3 of the Home Practice are in the Answer Key at the end of this lesson and at the end of this unit.

For her fractions Lee Yah wrote $\frac{23}{10}$ and 0.023 and said, "Twenty-three hundredths." Lee Yah said she should earn 3 points.

Jerome thought that Lee Yah was wrong, but he couldn't explain why. What do you think?

2. Luis and Ana were playing *Hundredths, Hundredths, Hundredths.* Ana made the following number.

   Write the common fraction and the decimal fraction for Ana's number.

3. When it was his turn, Luis made the following number.

   Write the common fraction and the decimal fraction for Luis's number.

4. Jessie and Roberto were playing *Hundredths, Hundredths, Hundredths.* Roberto made the following number.

   Write the common fraction and the decimal fraction for Roberto's number.

5. Jessie wanted to make 6.48. Use base-ten shorthand to show Jessie's number.

6. Roberto wanted to build the number 9.06. Use base-ten shorthand to show what pieces he should use.

7. Jessie wrote nine and six-hundredths like this: 9.6. Explain why this is incorrect.

Hundredths   SG • Grade 4 • Unit 10 • Lesson 3 **287**

Student Guide - page 287 (Answers on p. 77)

Assessment

- Use *Linda's Base-Ten Pieces* Assessment Blackline Master to assess students' understanding of decimal notation.

- Observe students as they work with the base-ten pieces to see if they can readily translate between concrete, pictorial, and symbolic representations of decimals. Record your observations on the *Observational Assessment Record*.

- The journal prompt can be used to assess students' understanding of the relationship between tenths and hundredths.

Journal Prompt

What are the trading rules for decimals? How many hundredths do you trade for one-tenth? How do decimal trading rules compare with whole number trading rules?

Name _____ Date _____

PART 3 Decimals

1. Numbers are represented in base-ten shorthand below. The flat is one whole. Label each of the following with its correct number. Then put the numbers in order from least to greatest.

A.

B.

C.

D.

2. Write a decimal for each of the following. Then, show your decimal using base-ten shorthand. The flat is one whole. Find a number that is:

   A. Between 8 and 9   B. Between 4 and 4.5

   C. Just a little bigger than 8   D. Between $\frac{1}{2}$ and 2

3. For each of the two problems below, put the measurements in order from shortest to longest.

   A. 0.6 m   23 cm   1 dm   0.45 m   55 dm

   B. 1.5 m   1 m and 8 dm   1.03 meter   1.24 meter

156 DAB · Grade 4 · Unit 10   USING DECIMALS

Discovery Assignment Book - page 156 (Answers on p. 77)

At a Glance

Math Facts and Daily Practice and Problems

DPP Bit I provides practice writing decimals using a number line (ruler). Tasks J and L are geometry items. Bits K and M provide math facts practice. For Challenge N, students convert units of time.

Part 1. Exploring Hundredths

1. Introduce the common fraction and the decimal fraction for one-hundredth using the vignette on the *Hundredths* Activity Pages in the *Student Guide.*
2. Use *Questions 1–16* to guide a class discussion.
3. Students use base-ten pieces to represent numbers using hundredths. Students write these numbers as common fractions and decimal fractions. *(Questions 4–8)*
4. Students translate between base-ten pieces, base-ten shorthand, and symbols for numbers to the nearest hundredth. *(Questions 9–16)*

Part 2. *Hundredths, Hundredths, Hundredths*

1. Introduce the game *Hundredths, Hundredths, Hundredths* by playing a demonstration game. Read the rules in the *Discovery Assignment Book.*
2. Students play the game in class. Students can make a recording chart or use the *Shorthand and Fractions Table* in the *Discovery Assignment Book.*

Part 3. *Linda's Base-Ten Pieces*

Review the Student Rubric: *Knowing* and ask students to complete the *Linda's Base-Ten Pieces* Assessment Blackline Master.

Homework

1. Assign the *More Hundredths* Activity Pages in the *Discovery Assignment Book* as homework after Part 1.
2. Assign the Homework section, *Playing Hundredths, Hundredths, Hundredths*, in the *Student Guide* after Part 2.
3. Assign Home Practice Part 3.

Assessment

1. Score the *Linda's Base-Ten Pieces* Assessment Blackline Master using the Knowing dimension of the *TIMS Multidimensional Rubric.*
2. Use the *Observational Assessment Record* to document students' abilities to translate between different representations of decimals.

Answer Key is on pages 74–79.

Notes:

Linda's Base-Ten Pieces

You need base-ten pieces (packs, flats, skinnies, and bits). A flat is one whole.

1. If a flat is 1, then what number is a pack?

2. If a flat is 1, then what number is a skinny?

3. If a flat is 1, then what number is a bit?

Linda has two base-ten pieces. She might have bits, skinnies, flats, or packs. For example, she might have two flats. She might have something else.

4. Find all the possible sets of pieces that Linda might have. Use base-ten shorthand to show each set she might have. Write the number for each set.

5. What is the largest number that Linda could possibly have?

6. What is the smallest number that Linda could possibly have?

7. Put the numbers that Linda could have in order from smallest to largest.

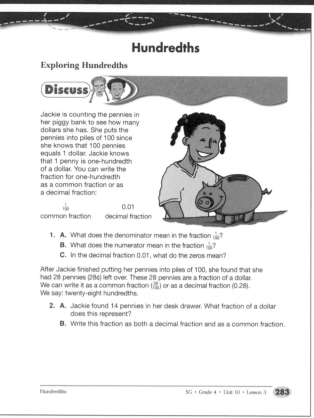

Hundredths

Exploring Hundredths

Jackie is counting the pennies in her piggy bank to see how many dollars she has. She puts the pennies into piles of 100 since she knows that 100 pennies equals 1 dollar. Jackie knows that 1 penny is one-hundredth of a dollar. You can write the fraction for one-hundredth as a common fraction or as a decimal fraction:

$\frac{1}{100}$ 0.01
common fraction   decimal fraction

1. **A.** What does the denominator mean in the fraction $\frac{1}{100}$?
   B. What does the numerator mean in the fraction $\frac{1}{100}$?
   C. In the decimal fraction 0.01, what do the zeros mean?

After Jackie finished putting her pennies into piles of 100, she found that she had 28 pennies (28¢) left over. These 28 pennies are a fraction of a dollar. We can write it as a common fraction ($\frac{28}{100}$) or as a decimal fraction (0.28). We say: twenty-eight hundredths.

2. **A.** Jackie found 14 pennies in her desk drawer. What fraction of a dollar does this represent?
   B. Write this fraction as both a decimal fraction and as a common fraction.

Hundredths   SG • Grade 4 • Unit 10 • Lesson 3   **283**

Student Guide - page 283

100 centimeters = 1 meter

3. **A.** Frank knows that there are 100 centimeters in a meter. That means that the length of one centimeter is 0.01 or $\frac{1}{100}$ of a meter. Frank's pencil is 15 cm long. What fraction of a meter is the length of the pencil?
   B. Write this fraction as both a decimal fraction and as a common fraction.

Irma wanted to use base-ten pieces to show hundredths. She learned in the last lesson that if a flat is 1 whole, then a skinny is 0.1 and a pack is 10.

 = 10   = 1   = 0.1

4. Which base-ten piece should Irma use to show one-hundredth? Explain why you chose the piece you did.

5. **A.** How many hundredths does a skinny represent? Write this number as a common fraction and as a decimal fraction.
   B. How many hundredths does a flat represent? Write this number as a common fraction and as a decimal fraction.

Nicholas used the following base-ten pieces to show a number. If a flat is one whole, then what number do these pieces represent?

These pieces show 3 wholes, 5 tenths, and 7 hundredths. We can write $3\frac{57}{100}$ or 3.57 for this number. We read both $3\frac{57}{100}$ and 3.57 as "three and fifty-seven hundredths."

6. **A.** Irma placed the following base-ten pieces on her desk. If a flat is one whole, then what number do these pieces represent?
   B. Write this number as a common fraction and as a decimal fraction.

284 SG • Grade 4 • Unit 10 • Lesson 3   Hundredths

Student Guide - page 284

Student Guide (p. 283)

Hundredths

1.***A.** A denominator of 100 means the whole is divided into 100 equal parts.

   B. A numerator of 1 means it is 1 of the equal parts.

   C. The 0 to the left of the decimal point in 0.01 means there are no wholes and the 0 to the right of the decimal point means there are no tenths.

2. **A.** fourteen-hundredths

   B. $\frac{14}{100}$ and 0.14 (Writing .14 is acceptable.)

Student Guide (p. 284)

3. **A.** fifteen-hundredths meter*

   B. $\frac{15}{100}$ and 0.15

4. A bit is used to show one-hundredth because 100 bits make a flat.*

5.***A.** 10 hundredths; $\frac{10}{100}$ and 0.10

   B. 100 hundredths; $\frac{100}{100}$ and 1.00 (or 1)

6. **A.** two and three-hundredths*

   B. $2\frac{3}{100}$ and 2.03

*Answers and/or discussion are included in the Lesson Guide.

Student Guide (p. 285)

7. 5.80 means five wholes, eight tenths, and no hundredths. 5.8 means five wholes and eight tenths. No hundredths is implied.

8. Answers will vary.

9. A.

B. :.:.·.·.·

C. /.....

D.

E.

10. A. 4.23 and $4\frac{23}{100}$ **B.** 2.57 and $2\frac{57}{100}$

C. 21.09 and $21\frac{9}{100}$ **D.** 20.3 and $20\frac{3}{10}$

7. Mrs. Dewey showed the following base-ten pieces to the class. She asked each student to record the number for these pieces.

Romesh recorded 5.80, and Jessie recorded 5.8. Explain why both students are correct.

8. Get a handful of mixed skinnies and bits and count them by hundredths. Count the skinnies first (ten-hundredths, twenty-hundredths, thirty-hundredths, etc.), and then count on for the bits. When you finish, write the number for your handful.

Explore

Tanya used the following base-ten pieces to show the number 3.67.

She recorded her work using base-ten shorthand.

9. Use base-ten pieces to make these numbers. Then, use base-ten shorthand to show what pieces you used. A flat is one whole.
   A. 2.34   **B.** 0.08   **C.** 0.15   **D.** 13.42   **E.** 3.04

10. Give a decimal number and a common fraction for the base-ten shorthand below:
   A.   **B.**

   C.   **D.**

Hundredths   SG • Grade 4 • Unit 10 • Lesson 3   **285**

Student Guide - page 285

11. A. Use base-ten pieces to make 0.1 and 0.2.

B. Use base-ten pieces to make a number more than 0.1 but less than 0.2. Use base-ten shorthand to show the pieces you used. Then write your number.

12. A. Use base-ten pieces to make 2.5 and 2.6.

B. Use base-ten pieces to make a number more than 2.5 but less than 2.6. Use base-ten shorthand to show the pieces you used. Then write your number.

For Questions 13–15, use base-ten shorthand to show how to make the number using the fewest base-ten pieces. Then write a decimal for the number.

13.

14.

15.

16. If you do not follow the fewest base-ten pieces rule, then the same number can be shown in several ways. Use base-ten pieces to make 0.42 in several ways. Use base-ten shorthand to show each way you find.

🎮 Homework

Playing *Hundredths, Hundredths, Hundredths*

Complete these questions after playing *Hundredths, Hundredths, Hundredths.*

1. Lee Yah and Jerome were playing *Hundredths, Hundredths, Hundredths.* Jerome tried to trick Lee Yah by making this number:

Student Guide - **page 286**

Student Guide (p. 286)

11. A. 1 and 11

B. Answers will vary.

12. A.

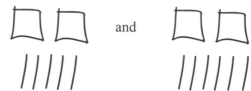 and

B. Answers will vary.

13. 1.83

14. 2.41

15. 10.17

16. Answers will vary.

Homework

1. Lee Yah is wrong because the 0 in the tenths' place in 0.023 means that there are no tenths. Since the twenty bits can be traded for two skinnies with 3 bits (3 hundredths) left over, the number should be written 0.23.

Student Guide (p. 287)

2. $2\frac{52}{100}$ and 2.52

3. $2\frac{91}{100}$ and 2.91

4. $\frac{54}{100}$ and 0.54

5.

6.

7. 9.6 means 9 wholes and 6 tenths, not 9 wholes and 6 hundredths.

Student Guide - page 287

Discovery Assignment Book (p. 156)

Home Practice*

Part 3. Decimals

1. **A.** 3.3 **B.** 3.6
   C. 3.03 **D.** 4.4
   3.03; 3.3; 3.6; 4.4

2. Answers will vary.

3. **A.** 1 dm, 23 cm, 0.45 m, 0.6 m, 55 dm
   B. 1.03 m, 1.24 m, 1.5 m, 1 m and 8 dm

Discovery Assignment Book - page 156

*Answers for all the Home Practice in the *Discovery Assignment Book* are at the end of the unit.

Discovery Assignment Book - page 173

Name _____ Date _____

More Hundredths

Making a Hundredths Chart

Professor Peabody made a hundredths chart. He forgot to fill in some of the chart. Help Professor Peabody by filling in the missing values.

0.01	0.02			0.06				0.1
	0.12		0.15			0.18		
0.21		0.24		0.27				
0.31		0.33		0.36				0.4
			0.45			0.48		
	0.52							
0.61			0.65				0.69	0.7
		0.73		0.76		0.79		
0.81					0.88			0.9
0.91		0.93			0.97			1

Use your completed chart to answer the following questions.

1. A. What number comes after 0.09?

   B. Why is it recorded as 0.1?

2. What number comes after 0.99?

3. Describe any patterns that you see in your hundredths chart.

Hundredths   DAB • Grade 4 • Unit 10 • Lesson 3 **173**

Discovery Assignment Book - page 174

Name _____ Date _____

4. Use base-ten shorthand to make these numbers.

   A. 19.06

   B. 0.68

   C. 1.73

   D. 44.4

5. Give a decimal fraction and a common fraction for the base-ten shorthand below:

   A.

   B.

   C.

   D.

   E.

174 DAB • Grade 4 • Unit 10 • Lesson 3   Hundredths

Discovery Assignment Book (pp. 173–174)

More Hundredths

1. A. 0.1

   B. 0.1 means there is one-tenth or 1 skinny. Since 1 skinny is equal to 10 bits, one-tenth is equal to ten-hundredths ($0.1 = 0.10$). Note that in the decimal 0.10, the one means there is one-tenth and the second zero means there are no hundredths.

2. 1.00 or 1

3. Answers will vary.

4. A.

   B.

   C.

   D.

5. A. $24\frac{37}{100}$ and 24.37

   B. $13\frac{9}{100}$ and 13.09

   C. $30\frac{3}{100}$ and 30.03

   D. $5\frac{3}{10}$ and 5.3

   E. $22\frac{22}{100}$ and 22.22

Unit Resource Guide (p. 73)

Linda's Base-Ten Pieces

I. 10

2. 0.1

3. 0.01

4.
 20

 11

 10.1

 10.01

 2

 1.1

 1.01

|| 0.2

| • 0.11

•• 0.02

5. 20

6. 0.02

7. 0.02, 0.11, 0.2, 1.01, 1.1, 2, 10.01, 10.1, 11, 20

Name _____ Date _____

Linda's Base-Ten Pieces

You need base-ten pieces (packs, flats, skinnies, and bits). A flat is one whole.

1. If a flat is 1, then what number is a pack?

2. If a flat is 1, then what number is a skinny?

3. If a flat is 1, then what number is a bit?

Linda has two base-ten pieces. She might have bits, skinnies, flats, or packs. For example, she might have two flats. She might have something else.

4. Find all the possible sets of pieces that Linda might have. Use base-ten shorthand to show each set she might have. Write the number for each set.

5. What is the largest number that Linda could possibly have?

6. What is the smallest number that Linda could possibly have?

7. Put the numbers that Linda could have in order from smallest to largest.

Assessment Blackline Master   URG • Grade 4 • Unit 10 • Lesson 3   73

Unit Resource Guide - page 73

Lesson 4

Downhill Racer

Estimated Class Sessions

4

Students roll cars down ramps to investigate the relationship between the height of the ramp and the distance a car travels after it leaves that ramp. This lab provides a context for students to use decimals and measure length in meters.

Key Content

- Identifying fixed variables in an experiment.
- Measuring length to the nearest hundredth of a meter.
- Collecting, organizing, graphing, and analyzing data.
- Using patterns in graphs to make predictions.
- Comparing and ordering decimals.

Key Vocabulary

- extrapolate
- fixed variables
- interpolate
- manipulated variable
- responding variable
- variables

Math Facts

DPP Bit Q provides practice with division facts.

Homework

1. Assign some or all of the questions in the Explore section for homework.
2. Assign the Homework section on the *Downhill Racer* Lab Pages after students complete the *Roberto's Data* Assessment Blackline Master.

Assessment

1. Use *Roberto's Data* Assessment Blackline Master to assess students' understanding of the *Downhill Racer* lab.
2. Use the *Observational Assessment Record* to document students' abilities to collect, organize, graph, and analyze data.
3. Transfer information from the Unit 10 *Observational Assessment Record* to students' *Individual Assessment Record Sheets*.

Curriculum Sequence

Before This Unit

Best-fit Lines

Students used best-fit lines to make predictions in Unit 5 Lesson 1 *Predictions from Graphs* and Lesson 4 *Bouncing Ball* lab. They also used best-fit lines in the lab *Volume vs. Number* in Unit 8.

Medians

Students used medians to average data collected in labs in Grades 1, 2, and 3. The median was reviewed in Unit 1 Lesson 3 *An Average Activity.* Students used averages in previous fourth-grade labs and activities. (The mean was introduced in Unit 5.)

TIMS Laboratory Method

Students used the TIMS Laboratory Method to collect, organize, graph, and analyze data in Units 1, 2, 5, and 8.

After This Unit

Best-fit Lines

Students will use graphs to make predictions in the labs *Plant Growth* and *Taste of TIMS* in Unit 15 and *Area vs. Length* in Unit 16. They will need to decide when it is appropriate to draw a best-fit line.

Medians

Students will continue to average data in labs and activities throughout the year. (See Units 13 and 15 for specific examples.)

TIMS Laboratory Method

Students will encounter labs in Units 14, 15, and 16.

Materials List

Supplies and Copies

Student	Teacher
Supplies for Each Student Group • wood or metal ramp at least 50 cm long • toy car or roller skate • 2–3 metersticks • 4–5 blocks or books of equal size • masking tape • calculator	**Supplies**
Copies • 1 copy of *Roberto's Data* per student (*Unit Resource Guide* Pages 95–96) • at least 3 copies of *Centimeter Graph Paper* per student (*Unit Resource Guide* Page 97) • 1 copy of *Three-trial Data Table* per student (*Unit Resource Guide* Page 98)	**Copies/Transparencies** • 1 transparency of *Centimeter Graph Paper* (*Unit Resource Guide* Page 97)

All blackline masters including assessment, transparency, and DPP masters are also on the Teacher Resource CD.

Student Books

Downhill Racer (*Student Guide* Pages 288–295)

Daily Practice and Problems and Home Practice

DPP items O–V (*Unit Resource Guide* Pages 24–28)

Note: Classrooms whose pacing differs significantly from the suggested pacing of the units should use the Math Facts Calendar in Section 4 of the *Facts Resource Guide* to ensure students receive the complete math facts program.

Assessment Tools

Observational Assessment Record (*Unit Resource Guide* Pages 13–14)
Individual Assessment Record Sheet (*Teacher Implementation Guide*, Assessment section)

O. Bit: Skip Counting (URG p. 24)

1. Skip count by dimes to $2.00.
   Start like this: $0.10, $0.20, $0.30 . . .
2. Skip count by tenths to 2.
   Start like this: 0.1, 0.2, 0.3 . . .
3. Skip count by quarters to $5.00.
   Start like this: $0.25, $0.50, $0.75 . . .
4. Skip count by 0.25 (twenty-five
   hundredths) to 5. Start like this:
   0.25, 0.50, 0.75 . . .

P. Task: Skip Counting by Tenths and Hundredths (URG p. 25)

1. Use a calculator to skip count by tenths.
   Skip count by tenths from 0 to 2.
   Press: $\boxed{0}\ \boxed{+}\ \boxed{.}\ \boxed{1}\ \boxed{=}\ \boxed{=}\ \boxed{=}$
   Say the numbers quietly to yourself.
2. Skip count by hundredths from 0 to
   one-tenth.
   Press: $\boxed{0}\ \boxed{+}\ \boxed{.}\ \boxed{0}\ \boxed{1}\ \boxed{=}\ \boxed{=}$
   Say the numbers quietly to yourself.
3. Skip count by tenths from 5 to 7.
   Press: $\boxed{5}\ \boxed{+}\ \boxed{.}\ \boxed{1}\ \boxed{=}\ \boxed{=}\ \boxed{=}$
   Say the numbers quietly to yourself.
4. Skip count by hundredths from 2 to 2.1.
   Press: $\boxed{2}\ \boxed{+}\ \boxed{.}\ \boxed{0}\ \boxed{1}\ \boxed{=}\ \boxed{=}$
   Say the numbers quietly to yourself.

Q. Bit: More Fact Families for × and ÷ (URG p. 26)

The following four facts are in the same
fact family.

$4 \times 3 = 12$ $3 \times 4 = 12$
$12 \div 3 = 4$ $12 \div 4 = 3$

Solve each pair of related number sentences. Then
give two other facts in the same fact family.

A. $7 \times 2 = ?$ and $14 \div 7 = ?$
B. $2 \times 3 = ?$ and $6 \div 2 = ?$
C. $3 \times 8 = ?$ and $24 \div 3 = ?$
D. $6 \times 3 = ?$ and $18 \div 3 = ?$
E. $4 \times 2 = ?$ and $8 \div 4 = ?$
F. $3 \times 8 = ?$ and $24 \div 8 = ?$
G. $3 \times 1 = ?$ and $3 \div 1 = ?$

R. Task: Ordering Decimals (URG p. 26)

1. Draw each of the following numbers in base-ten
   shorthand. The flat is one whole. Then put the
   numbers in order from smallest to largest:
   0.4   0.39   0.41   0.5   1.00
2. Draw each of the following numbers in
   base-ten shorthand. The flat is one whole.
   Then put these numbers in order from
   smallest to largest:
   0.09   0.8   1.0   0.27   0.01

Daily Practice and Problems

Suggestions for using the DPPs are on page 92.

S. Bit: Write a Decimal (URG p. 27)

1. Write a decimal:
   A. between 7 and 8
   B. between 1 and 2
   C. just a little bigger than 4
   D. just a little less than 2
   E. between $\frac{1}{2}$ and 0.8
   F. between 5 and 5.5

2. Explain your strategy for Question E.

T. Task: Which Length Is Longer?
(URG p. 27)

1. Use a meterstick to help you answer the following.
   (Bits and skinnies might help, too. Remember, one bit is one centimeter long. One skinny is 10 cm or 1 decimeter long.) Which is longer:
   A. 2 cm or 11 mm?
   B. 32 mm or 3 cm?
   C. 5 dm or 45 cm?
   D. 2 m or 180 cm?
   E. 3 dm or 300 mm?
   F. 87 cm or 8 dm?

2. Choose one of the questions and explain your strategy for solving it.

U. Bit: Smallest, Largest, and In-Between (URG p. 28)

For the following base-ten shorthand, the flat is one whole.

A. Which is the smallest?
B. Which is the largest?
C. Which are equal?
D. Write numbers for each and put them in order from smallest to largest. (The flat is one whole.)

V. Task: Metric Conversions
(URG p. 28)

Change each of these lengths to meters.
(*Hint:* Think of metersticks, skinnies, and bits.)

A. 327 cm	B. 405 cm
C. 5 cm	D. 87 cm
E. 10 dm	F. 24 dm

Change each of these lengths to centimeters.

G. 1.1 m	H. 1.01 m
I. 4 dm	J. 4.1 dm
K. 3.27 m	L. 0.4 dm

Ask students to bring toy cars and roller skates (not in-line skates) to class for this lab. All cars should be tested prior to beginning the lab. The lab requires cars that roll straight for consistent distances. The floor where the cars are rolled should be level without cracks or bumps.

A primary goal of this lab is for students to practice controlling variables. Many things can affect the distance the cars roll: type of car, height of ramp, exact location of the ramp in the room (since some parts of the floor may be bumpier than other parts), position of the starting line on the ramp, how the car is released, and "accidents" (e.g., bumping the side of the ramp). Of all these variables, only the ramp height is allowed to change; the others must stay fixed.

For this reason and to help students stay focused during the lab, they should be familiar with the equipment before they begin. The following steps can help:

1. Students bring in cars from home several days before the activity.

2. Set up a ramp area (or two) with inclines, blocks, or books, and metersticks.

3. Let the children play with the cars informally during free time for a few days. You might suggest a "roll-off" during recess.

4. Ask the students to identify "good rollers." A good roller will roll straight for about 2 meters or more.

TIMS Tip

If a large area such as the gym or playground is not available or if you do not have a ramp for each group, then you can set up a smaller number of ramps. Students can draw their pictures or work on DPP items while they wait for their group's turn to collect data.

5. Discuss *"What variables affect how far a car rolls?"*

Figure 6: *Ramp setup*

DPP item O provides practice skip counting by 0.1s and 0.25s. This item will prepare students for scaling their graphs.

Teaching the Lab

This lab uses the TIMS Laboratory Method: beginning the investigation, gathering and organizing the data, graphing the data, and analyzing the results.

Part 1 **Beginning the Investigation**

One way to introduce the lab is to set up two ramps, one held up by two blocks or books, the other held up by four blocks or books. Show students the car that will be rolled down both ramps.

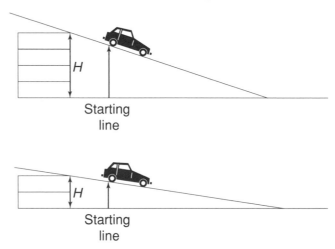

Figure 7: *Racing areas with different heights*

Ask:

- *What is the same in these two racing areas?* (The type of ramp and the type of car.)
- *What is different?* (One ramp is higher.)
- *If I release the car on each ramp, how far will the car roll on the floor? Which ramp will make the car roll farther?* The role of variables like the starting point, the kind of car, the manner of release, and so on, can be highlighted by manipulating this setup.

Introduce the lab using the *Downhill Racer* Lab Pages in the *Student Guide.* Explain that instead of using the steps from Jackie's apartment building, the class will use books or blocks to investigate the relationship between the height of a ramp and how far a car rolls.

To investigate the effect changing the height has on the distance the car rolls, all other variables involved in the experiment should be held fixed. In planning the experiment, students should discuss these variables *(Question 2)*:

- car (Each group should use the same car throughout.)
- type of floor (Each ramp should remain in the same location throughout.)
- method of releasing the car (The back wheels should be placed on the starting line and the car should be released gently without being pushed. Do not use spring-loaded cars.)
- position of the stack of blocks or books where the height (*H*) is measured (at the same place under the ramp)
- how far the starting line is from the bottom of the ramp (Before students collect the data, they should adjust the starting line so the car rolls a reasonable amount. Then they should mark it with tape.)
- how the distance rolled (*D*) is measured (from the bottom of the ramp to the back wheel of the car)

Manipulated and Responding Variables. The **manipulated variable** *(Question 4)* is the variable with values we select at the beginning of the experiment. In this lab it is the height of the ramp (*H*). Either you select the heights or let the students select them. In any case, the values should be chosen so the cars will roll a reasonable distance, yet not too far. Try out different heights using different numbers of books or blocks that are the same thickness. The values should be well-spaced for easy graphing and preferably in some proportional pattern. Values like *H* = 4 cm, 8 cm, 12 cm or *H* = 4 cm, 16 cm, 24 cm work well. For example, you could use 1, 2, and 4 geography books or 2, 4, and 6 spelling books to get the desired heights in cm.

The **responding variable** *(Question 5)* is the variable with values we find during the experiment. Here it is the distance the car rolls on the floor (*D*). After the car stops, students should measure the distance from the bottom edge of the incline to the rear

Downhill Racer

Jackie and her brother Derrick want to play with their toy cars. They set up a ramp using the steps in front of their apartment building and a thick board.

Jackie suggested using a meterstick to find how far each car traveled. Derrick wondered, "Will the cars roll different distances if we put the ramp on different steps?"

> I think the cars will roll farther with the ramp on a higher step.

288   SG • Grade 4 • Unit 10 • Lesson 4   Downhill Racer

Student Guide - page 288

1. Do you think a car will roll farther when the ramp is set up on a higher step? Explain why you think so.

Jackie and Derrick did an experiment to find out how far each car rolled when the ramp was put on steps of different heights. First, they talked about how to be sure that the experiment was fair. Derrick suggested that the starting line on the ramp should stay the same.

2. What other variables should not change during the experiment? Why?

3. Jackie and Derrick decided to run three trials for each different height. Why was this a good idea?

Use the TIMS Laboratory Method to do an experiment like Jackie and Derrick's. Use a car and a ramp to study the relationship between the height of the ramp (*H*) and the distance your car will roll on the ground (*D*).

Use blocks or books to change the height of the ramp. The height (*H*) is the height of the blocks (or books). The blocks should touch the ramp at the same place for the entire experiment. The distance (*D*) should be measured from the bottom of the ramp to the back wheels of the car.

4. What is the manipulated variable?

5. What is the responding variable?

Draw a picture of the lab. Be sure to show the two main variables, Height (*H*) and Distance (*D*). Also show the length of your ramp and where your starting line is.

6. Later, you will make and check predictions about how far your car rolls. Unless you are careful now, you may not be able to check your predictions later. Write a paragraph that describes exactly how you set up your lab, so that later you can set it up again in exactly the same way. (*Hint:* Look at your answer to Question 2.)

Downhill Racer   SG • Grade 4 • Unit 10 • Lesson 4   289

Student Guide - page 289 *(Answers on p. 99)*

7. **A.** Work with your group to do the experiment.
   - Discuss what values for the height (*H*) you will use.
   - Measure the height in centimeters.
   - Measure the distance (*D*) the car rolls to the nearest hundredth of a meter. Use decimals to record your measurements of this distance.
   - Do three trials for each height. Average the three distances for each height by finding the median distance.
   - Keep track of your data in a table like this one:

H Ramp Height (in cm)	*D* Distance Rolled (in m)			
	Trial 1	Trial 2	Trial 3	Average

   B. Why is it a good idea to find the average distance?

Graph

8. **A.** Plot your data points on *Centimeter Graph Paper*. Put the manipulated variable on the horizontal axis. Put the responding variable on the vertical axis. Remember to title your graph, label axes, and record units. Before you scale your axes, discuss with your group how much room you need on your graph for extrapolation. (*Hint:* Look at Questions 9–12.)

   B. Look at your points on your graph. Do the points lie close to a straight line? If so, use a ruler to fit a line to the points. Extend the line in both directions.

Student Guide - page 290 *(Answers on p. 99)*

wheels of the car, as shown in Figure 8. Students should measure this distance to the nearest hundredth of a meter and use decimals to express it.

Pictures. After you discuss the lab and students understand the procedures, they draw pictures of the investigation. Emphasize that a good picture shows the equipment, identifies the variables, and communicates the procedures. Students' pictures can help you judge who is ready to go on to the next phase—gathering data. The picture in Figure 9 shows the experimental setup and the two main variables labeled *H* and *D*. However, it does not clearly show the method for measuring the distance—from the end of the ramp to the rear wheels.

Part 2 **Gathering and Organizing the Data**

Multiple Trials. Discuss how many trials should be made for each height. The data table shown in the *Student Guide* allows for three trials, but you can make a different number if you prefer. The important point is to make multiple trials.

Discuss bad trials, as when the car rolls off the side of the ramp. Ask whether including such trials would be fair. Help students understand why they should discard these trials. All measurements for trials with the same height should have distances that are close to one another.

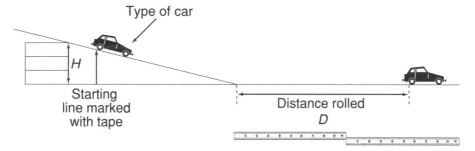

Figure 8: *Measuring the height (H) and the distance (D)*

Figure 9: *A student picture*

Setting up the Ramps. Ideally, the cars should roll at least two meters at the maximum height, so students should try a variety of starting points before they begin to gather their data. They may notice that if they start at the top of the ramp, the car rolls too far or takes a bad roll. Students should mark the ramp with a piece of masking tape so the starting point is the same each time. *Question 6* asks students to describe their setups as precisely as possible so later they can check their predictions using exactly the same setups.

Once all the trials are done, students find the average distance rolled. They should use the median since they have not yet calculated with decimals. Finding the median also provides a good opportunity for them to order decimals. In *Question 7B,* they are asked why taking an average is a good idea. So much can go wrong in any experiment that repeated measurements are crucial. Due to small errors, we average the data to get the most accurate result; averaging reduces the effect of random errors we cannot control.

Part 3 Graphing the Data and Analyzing the Results

Deciding how much room to leave for extrapolation is not easy. No exact rule can be given, only that *some* room should be allowed. Questions later in the lab ask about ramp heights up to 16 cm. Numbering the horizontal axis to 30 cm should suffice. Numbering the vertical axis will depend on the longest distance available for the car to roll. Students may need help scaling the vertical axis using decimals. See Figure 11. (DPP Item O will prepare students for scaling their graphs.)

Questions 9–11 explore interpolation, extrapolation, and predicting. Students should mark their predictions on the graph as shown in Figure 11. They should then check their predictions experimentally. For students' predictions to be close, the experimental setups must be the same—all variables must be held fixed except the height of the ramp.

H Ramp Height (in cm)	D Distance Rolled (in m)			
	Trial 1	Trial 2	Trial 3	Average
4 cm	1.23 m	1.25 m	1.23 m	1.23 m
8 cm	2.56 m	2.52 m	2.54 m	2.54 m
12 cm	3.67 m	3.71 m	3.64 m	3.67 m

Figure 10: *A student data table (averages are medians)*

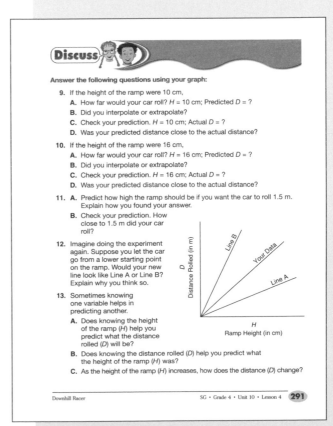

Discuss

Answer the following questions using your graph:

9. If the height of the ramp were 10 cm,
   A. How far would your car roll? *H* = 10 cm; Predicted *D* = ?
   B. Did you interpolate or extrapolate?
   C. Check your prediction. *H* = 10 cm; Actual *D* = ?
   D. Was your predicted distance close to the actual distance?

10. If the height of the ramp were 16 cm,
   A. How far would your car roll? *H* = 16 cm; Predicted *D* = ?
   B. Did you interpolate or extrapolate?
   C. Check your prediction. *H* = 16 cm; Actual *D* = ?
   D. Was your predicted distance close to the actual distance?

11. A. Predict how high the ramp should be if you want the car to roll 1.5 m. Explain how you found your answer.
   B. Check your prediction. How close to 1.5 m did your car roll?

12. Imagine doing the experiment again. Suppose you let the car go from a lower starting point on the ramp. Would your new line look like Line A or Line B? Explain why you think so.

13. Sometimes knowing one variable helps in predicting another.
   A. Does knowing the height of the ramp (*H*) help you predict what the distance rolled (*D*) will be?
   B. Does knowing the distance rolled (*D*) help you predict what the height of the ramp (*H*) was?
   C. As the height of the ramp (*H*) increases, how does the distance (*D*) change?

Downhill Racer   SG • Grade 4 • Unit 10 • Lesson 4   **291**

Student Guide - page 291 (Answers on p. 100)

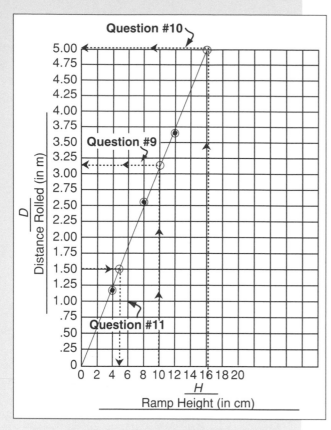

Figure 11: *Predictions on student's graph*

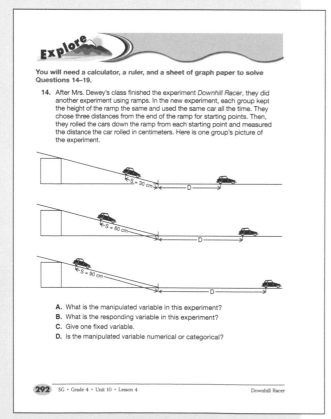

Student Guide - page 292 *(Answers on p. 100)*

In *Questions 9D, 10D,* and *11B,* ask if students' predictions are close. Help students decide if their predictions are close. (Even students who completed Unit 6 Lesson 5 need not use the 10% standard in this lab because they have not had experience with decimal computation.) Students should understand that "closeness" is relative. The difference between predicted distances and actual measurements can be greater for longer distances than shorter distances. For example, a prediction of 5 m can be considered close if the actual measurement is within 0.5 m. However, a predicted distance of 1 m would not be considered close if the actual distance the car rolled was 0.5 m or 1.5 m, but it would be if the rolling distance were between 0.9 m and 1.1 m.

For *Question 11B,* you might ask a limited number of students to check their predictions.

In *Question 12,* one fixed variable is changed: the starting point on the ramp is lowered. The car does not build up as much speed and therefore will not roll as far. The new graph would look like Line A.

Content Note

Why Does the Car Roll and Stop? It is gravity that pulls the car down the incline and friction that stops it. If the release point is lowered, gravity does not act for as long a time and the car will not go as far.

Part 4 **Explore Questions**

Questions 14–19 review several concepts developed in Grade 4. In the context of a slight variation on the *Downhill Racer* lab, students identify different types of variables, graph data, make predictions when changing one variable, and find both kinds of averages. Students may work on the problems individually or in groups, as class work or as homework. Students will need calculators and *Centimeter Graph Paper*.

The focus of the problems is an experiment similar to *Downhill Racer,* but the height of the ramp stays the same and the starting point on the ramp changes. *Question 14* requires students to use their knowledge of variables to identify manipulated, responding, and fixed variables and to distinguish between numerical and categorical variables.

Compare the variables in this situation with those in the lab the students just completed. Ask:

- *What was the manipulated variable in the Downhill Racer lab?* (Height of the incline)
- *What kind of a variable is height in **Question 14**?* (Fixed)
- *What is the manipulated variable in **Question 14**?* (Starting point of the car)
- *What kind of variable was the starting point in the Downhill Racer lab?* (Fixed)
- *What are some other variables that could be investigated by making them the manipulated variable?* (Students may suggest the size of car, type of wheels on the car, floor surface, or surface of the incline. Have students make conjectures about what they would find out by making any one of these variables the manipulated variable.)

Questions 15 and *16* ask students to find both medians and means of a given set of data and to give their answers to the nearest centimeter. Students graph a set of data and use the graph to make predictions using interpolation and extrapolation in *Questions 17–19*.

---

15. John's group rolled its car down the ramp three times from the starting point that was 60 cm from the end of the ramp. Here are the distances the car rolled for three trials: 83 cm, 84 cm, and 89 cm.
    A. Find the mean distance for these trials. Give your answer to the nearest centimeter.
    B. Find the median distance.

16. Nila's group chose to do four trials. Here are the distances the car rolled from a starting point that was 120 cm from the end of the ramp: 189 cm, 177 cm, 186 cm, and 188 cm.
    A. Find the mean distance for these trials.
    B. Find the median distance. Give your answer to the nearest centimeter.

17. Here is Shannon's data. Make a graph of the data.

Shannon's Data

H Starting Distance From End of Ramp (in cm)	D Distance Rolled (in cm)			
	Trial 1	Trial 2	Trial 3	Average
30	48	47	47	47
60	87	84	86	86
90	144	142	145	144

Student Guide - page 293 (Answers on p. 101)

---

18. A. Shannon uses the same lab setup. She starts to roll the car down the ramp 45 cm from the end of the ramp. Use your graph to predict the distance the car will roll.
    B. Did you use interpolation or extrapolation to find your answer?

19. A. Shannon uses the same lab setup. She starts to roll the car down the ramp 120 cm from the end of the ramp. Use your graph to predict the distance the car will roll.
    B. Did you use interpolation or extrapolation to find your answer?

Student Guide - page 294 (Answers on p. 101)

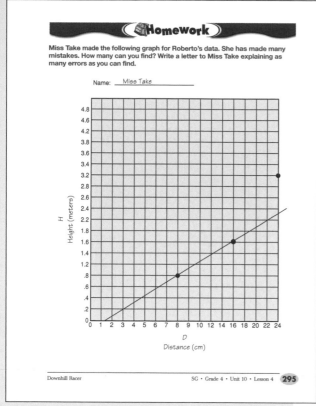

Math Facts

DPP Bit Q provides practice with division facts using fact families.

Homework and Practice

- Assign for homework some or all of ***Questions 14–19*** in the Explore section of the *Student Guide*. These problems review the concepts and procedures developed in this lab and previous labs. (Students will need a piece of *Centimeter Graph Paper*.)

- DPP items O and P provide practice skip counting with decimals. Items R, S, and U develop number sense with decimals. Items T and V provide practice with metric measurement.

- In the Homework section, students are asked to find errors in Miss Take's graph of Roberto's data. Accordingly, this homework must be assigned after students have completed the *Roberto's Data* Assessment Blackline Master. Sample student work is shown in Figure 12.

  Notice that Ana identified errors on the axes, both in scaling and labeling. She also recognized that the data points were not plotted correctly. Miss Take did not accurately determine where the average distances of 0.95 m, 1.79 m, and 2.97 lie along the vertical axis. Ana also demonstrated knowledge of how to draw a best-fit line through a set of data points.

Dear Miss Take,
     I wanted to inform you that when you made the graph for Roberto, you made some mistakes. For one thing you forgot the title. Then on the horizontal axis you counted up to ten by ones, then you went by twos untill the end. On the vertical axis you counted by twos, but you forgot 1.0, 2.0, 3.0, and 4.0, and 5.0. Also on the vertical axis. Roberto didn't do his height by meters, he did it in centimeters. It's a big difference, actually by 99 cm!
     Now I would like explain that when you make a best fit line you don't pick two dots and make a line between them. You should seperate the dots with the line making sure at least one dot is on each side, but a dot may be on the line. Also you incorrectly rounded the distances and labeled the horizontal axis in cm and it should be m. Plus, the words distance and height are in each others places. Now Miss Take, it's alright to make a little guess on where you put the dot. Nice speaking to you.
                       Sincerely,
                       Ana

Figure 12: *Sample student work for the Homework in the* Student Guide

Assessment

- In *Roberto's Data* Assessment Blackline Master students are given sample data for *Downhill Racer* to graph and analyze. Use this exercise to assess how well students can measure and graph decimals and how well they understand the meaning of the lab *Downhill Racer.* Students will need a copy of *Centimeter Graph Paper* to complete the assessment.

- Use the *Observational Assessment Record* to document students' progress in conducting experiments using the TIMS Laboratory Method. Note how well students collect data. In particular, note how well they keep appropriate variables fixed.

- Transfer information from the Unit 10 *Observational Assessment Record* to students' *Individual Assessment Record Sheets.*

At a Glance

Math Facts and Daily Practice and Problems

DPP Bit Q practices division facts. Items O, P, R, S, and U all provide practice with decimals and build number sense. Items T and V build decimal understanding through metric measurement.

Before the Lab

Students bring in toy cars and roller skates. They select good rollers to use in the experiment.

Part 1. Beginning the Investigation

1. Set up two ramps with different heights to begin the lab discussion.
2. Introduce Jackie and Derrick's experiment by reading together the first page of the *Downhill Racer* Lab Pages in the *Student Guide.*
3. Discuss *Questions 1–3* in the *Student Guide,* which will guide students in planning their experiment. Include fixed variables in your discussion. *(Question 2)*
4. Students identify the manipulated and responding variables in the experiment. *(Questions 4* and *5)*
5. Students draw pictures of the lab setup. They should indicate key variables.

Part 2. Gathering and Organizing the Data

1. Set up as many ramps as space and materials allow.
2. Students work in groups of three to four to collect their data. *(Question 6)*
3. They record their data on a copy of a *Three-trial Data Table. (Question 7A)*
4. Discuss why taking an average of the data for the three trials is a good idea. *(Question 7B)*

Part 3. Graphing the Data and Analyzing the Results

1. Students graph their data on a copy of *Centimeter Graph Paper. (Question 8)*
2. Students use their data to answer *Questions 9–11.* These questions require predictions to be checked, which may require using the ramps again.

Part 4. Explore Questions

Students complete *Questions 14–19* individually or in small groups.

Homework

1. Assign some or all of the questions in the Explore section for homework.
2. Assign the Homework section on the *Downhill Racer* Lab Pages after students complete the *Roberto's Data* Assessment Blackline Master.

Assessment

1. Use *Roberto's Data* Assessment Blackline Master to assess students' understanding of the *Downhill Racer* lab.
2. Use the *Observational Assessment Record* to document students' abilities to collect, organize, graph, and analyze data.
3. Transfer information from the Unit 10 *Observational Assessment Record* to students' *Individual Assessment Record Sheets.*

Answer Key is on pages 99–103.

Notes:

Roberto's Data

You will need a sheet of *Centimeter Graph Paper* and a ruler.

Roberto did *Downhill Racer.* This is his data:

H Ramp Height (in cm)	D Distance Rolled (in m)			
	Trial 1	Trial 2	Trial 3	Average
8	0.97	0.93	0.95	
16	1.75	1.79	1.80	
24	3.01	2.97	2.90	

1. Find the median distance (*D*) for each height. Write your answers in the table.

2. Why did Roberto carry out three trials for each height?

3. Graph Roberto's data. Remember a title, labels, and units.

4. Fit a line to Roberto's data.

Use your graph of Roberto's data to answer these questions:

5. If the ramp height were 4 cm, how far would Roberto's car roll?

6. If the ramp height were 20 cm, how far would Roberto's car roll?

7. If Roberto's car rolled 2.5 m, what was the height of the ramp?

8. Roberto wants his car to roll 3.5 meters. What should Roberto do so that his car rolls 3.5 meters?

9. Roberto's friend Keenya used Roberto's car and ramp to collect her data. Keenya moved her starting line higher than Roberto's. Do you think Keenya's car rolled farther than Roberto's? Why or why not?

10. What do you think Keenya's graph would look like? Would her line be above or below Roberto's? Draw a line on your graph and label it "Keenya's Data."

Assessment Blackline Master

Name _____   Date _____

Centimeter Graph Paper, Blackline Master

_____

	Trial 1	Trial 2	Trial 3	Average

Three-trial Data Table, Blackline Master

Student Guide (p. 289)

1. Answers will vary.

2. See the list of fixed variables in Lesson Guide 4. Car, ramp surface, floor surface, starting line, measuring points, etc.*

3. Three or more trials for each height is a good idea since experimental and measurement errors as well as mistakes are inevitable. Gross errors can be checked. If the distance for one trial is very different from the other trials, that data should be thrown out and the trial should be repeated.

4. the height (*H*) of the ramp*

5. the distance (*D*) the car rolls*

6. Answers will vary, but paragraphs should include all the variables students hold fixed in order to make the experiment fair. For example, each group should describe the car they use, the starting line on their ramp, etc.

1. Do you think a car will roll farther when the ramp is set up on a higher step? Explain why you think so.

Jackie and Derrick did an experiment to find out how far each car rolled when the ramp was put on steps of different heights. First, they talked about how to be sure that the experiment was fair. Derrick suggested that the starting line on the ramp should stay the same.

2. What other variables should not change during the experiment? Why?

3. Jackie and Derrick decided to run three trials for each different height. Why was this a good idea?

Use the TIMS Laboratory Method to do an experiment like Jackie and Derrick's. Use a car and a ramp to study the relationship between the height of the ramp (*H*) and the distance your car will roll on the ground (*D*).

Use blocks or books to change the height of the ramp. The height (*H*) is the height of the blocks (or books). The blocks should touch the ramp at the same place for the entire experiment. The distance (*D*) should be measured from the bottom of the ramp to the back wheels of the car.

4. What is the manipulated variable?

5. What is the responding variable?

Draw a picture of the lab. Be sure to show the two main variables, Height (*H*) and Distance (*D*). Also show the length of your ramp and where your starting line is.

6. Later, you will make and check predictions about how far your car rolls. Unless you are careful now, you may not be able to check your predictions later. Write a paragraph that describes exactly how you set up your lab, so that later you can set it up again in exactly the same way. (*Hint:* Look at your answer to Question 2.)

Downhill Racer   SG • Grade 4 • Unit 10 • Lesson 4   **289**

Student Guide - page 289

Student Guide (p. 290)

7.* A. See Figure 10 in Lesson Guide 4.

   B. It is a good idea to find the average distance to average out any experimental and measurement error.

8. See Figure 11 in Lesson Guide 4.

7. A. Work with your group to do the experiment.
   • Discuss what values for the height (*H*) you will use.
   • Measure the height in centimeters.
   • Measure the distance (*D*) the car rolls to the nearest hundredth of a meter. Use decimals to record your measurements of this distance.
   • Do three trials for each height. Average the three distances for each height by finding the median distance.
   • Keep track of your data in a table like this one:

H Ramp Height (in cm)	*D* Distance Rolled (in m)			
	Trial 1	Trial 2	Trial 3	Average

   B. Why is it a good idea to find the average distance?

8. A. Plot your data points on *Centimeter Graph Paper.* Put the manipulated variable on the horizontal axis. Put the responding variable on the vertical axis. Remember to title your graph, label axes, and record units. Before you scale your axes, discuss with your group how much room you need on your graph for extrapolation. (*Hint:* Look at Questions 9–12.)

   B. Look at your points on the graph. Do the points lie close to a straight line? If so, use a ruler to fit a line to the points. Extend the line in both directions.

290   SG • Grade 4 • Unit 10 • Lesson 4   Downhill Racer

Student Guide - page 290

*Answers and/or discussion are included in the Lesson Guide.

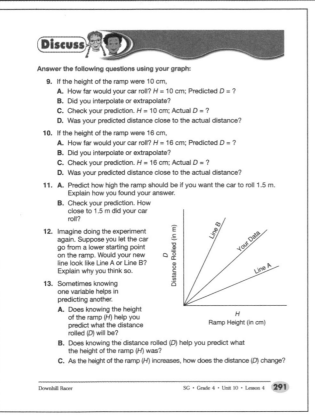

Student Guide - page 291

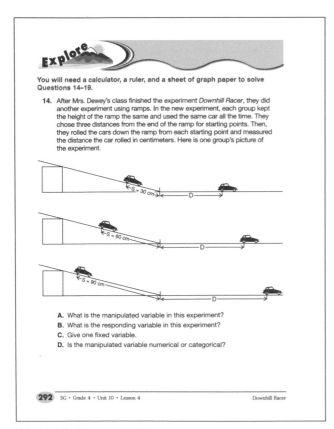

Student Guide - page 292

Student Guide (p. 291)

Answers to *Questions 9–12* are based on the sample data and graph in Lesson Guide 4. Students' answers will vary based on their data.

9. **A.** Predicted $D = 3.15$ m

   B. interpolate

   C. Answers will vary.

   D. Answers will vary.*

10. **A.** 5 m

    B. extrapolate

    C. Answers will vary.

    D. Answers will vary.*

11. **A.** 5 cm. Find 1.5 cm on the vertical axis of the graph; draw a line horizontally until it reaches the best-fit line; draw a vertical line down until it reaches the horizontal axis. The point (5 cm) at which the vertical line touches the horizontal axis is the predicted height of the ramp.

    B. Answers will vary.*

12. Line A. If the starting point were lower on the ramp, the car would not travel as far and the line would not be as steep as the line for the experiment.*

13. **A.** Yes

    B. Yes

    C. The distance increases.

Student Guide (p. 292)

14. **A.** Starting Distance (S)

    B. Distance the car rolls (D)

    C. Possible answers: height of the ramp, car

    D. numerical

*Answers and/or discussion are included in the Lesson Guide.

Student Guide (p. 293)

15. **A.** 85 cm

    B. 84 cm

16. **A.** 185 cm

    B. 187 cm

17.

Shannon's Data

Starting Distance in cm

Student Guide (p. 294)

18. **A.** About 70 cm. (Answers may vary slightly due to differences in best-fit lines and scales.)

    B. interpolation

19. **A.** About 180 cm. (Answers may vary somewhat due to differences in best-fit lines and scales.)

    B. extrapolation

15. John's group rolled its car down the ramp three times from the starting point that was 60 cm from the end of the ramp. Here are the distances the car rolled for three trials: 83 cm, 84 cm, and 89 cm.
    A. Find the mean distance for these trials. Give your answer to the nearest centimeter.
    B. Find the median distance.

16. Nila's group chose to do four trials. Here are the distances the car rolled from a starting point that was 120 cm from the end of the ramp: 189 cm, 177 cm, 186 cm, and 188 cm.
    A. Find the mean distance for these trials.
    B. Find the median distance. Give your answer to the nearest centimeter.

17. Here is Shannon's data. Make a graph of the data.

Shannon's Data

H Starting Distance From End of Ramp (in cm)	D Distance Rolled (in cm)			
	Trial 1	Trial 2	Trial 3	Average
30	48	47	47	47
60	87	84	86	86
90	144	142	145	144

Student Guide - page 293

18. **A.** Shannon uses the same lab setup. She starts to roll the car down the ramp 45 cm from the end of the ramp. Use your graph to predict the distance the car will roll.
    B. Did you use interpolation or extrapolation to find your answer?

19. **A.** Shannon uses the same lab setup. She starts to roll the car down the ramp 120 cm from the end of the ramp. Use your graph to predict the distance the car will roll.
    B. Did you use interpolation or extrapolation to find your answer?

Student Guide - page 294

*Answers and/or discussion are included in the Lesson Guide.

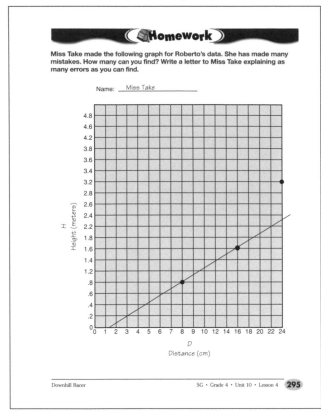

Student Guide - page 295

Student Guide (p. 295)

Homework

Student paragraphs should include descriptions of the following mistakes:

- The horizontal axis should be labeled with Height (H), not Distance (D).

- The vertical axis should be labeled with Distance (D).

- There is no title.

- The points from Roberto's data are plotted incorrectly.

- The best-fit line is incorrect. It should take into account the point for $H = 24$ cm. The line should go above the two lower points and below the third point.

- The horizontal axis is scaled by ones to 10, then is scaled by twos.

- The vertical axis scale is missing 1.0, 2.0, 3.0, 4.0, and 4.4.

Unit Resource Guide (pp. 95–96)

Roberto's Data

1. Data table averages:
    0.95
    1.79
    2.97

2. Answers will vary. Roberto carried out 3 trials to check for mistakes in data collection and to average out small errors.

3.–4.

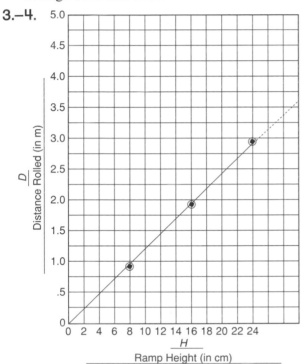

5. 0.5 m (Answers may vary somewhat due to differences in best-fit lines and scales.)

6. 2.4 m (Answers may vary slightly due to differences in best-fit lines and scales.)

7. 21 cm

8. Roberto should raise the ramp to about 29 cm.

9. A higher starting line would allow the car to start at a greater height and roll longer, so the car will roll farther.

10. Keenya's line will be above Roberto's.

Name _____ Date _____

Roberto's Data

You will need a sheet of *Centimeter Graph Paper* and a ruler.

Roberto did Downhill Racer. This is his data:

H Ramp Height (in cm)	D Distance Rolled (in m)			
	Trial 1	Trial 2	Trial 3	Average
8	0.97	0.93	0.95	
16	1.75	1.79	1.80	
24	3.01	2.97	2.90	

1. Find the median distance (*D*) for each height. Write your answers in the table.

2. Why did Roberto carry out three trials for each height?

3. Graph Roberto's data. Remember a title, labels, and units.

4. Fit a line to Roberto's data.

Use your graph of Roberto's data to answer these questions:

5. If the ramp height were 4 cm, how far would Roberto's car roll?

6. If the ramp height were 20 cm, how far would Roberto's car roll?

Unit Resource Guide - page 95

Name _____ Date _____

7. If Roberto's car rolled 2.5 m, what was the height of the ramp?

8. Roberto wants his car to roll 3.5 meters. What should Roberto do so that his car rolls 3.5 meters?

9. Roberto's friend Keenya used Roberto's car and ramp to collect her data. Keenya moved her starting line higher than Roberto's. Do you think Keenya's car rolled farther than Roberto's? Why or why not?

10. What do you think Keenya's graph would look like? Would her line be above or below Roberto's? Draw a line on your graph and label it "Keenya's Data."

Unit Resource Guide - page 96

Decimal Hex

Lesson Overview

Estimated Class Sessions

1

Students move two tokens to travel across a game board by correctly comparing two decimal fractions or a decimal and a common fraction.

Key Content

- Comparing and ordering decimal fractions.
- Translating between a common and a decimal fraction.

Homework

Students take home the *Decimal Hex* Game Pages to play the game with family members.

Assessment

Use the *Observational Assessment Record* to note students' abilities to compare and order decimals.

In Grade 3 Unit 15, students were introduced to this game.

Materials List

Supplies and Copies

Student	Teacher
Supplies for Each Student • 2 same-color centimeter cubes as game markers • clear plastic spinner or paper clip and pencil • base-ten pieces	**Supplies**
Copies	**Copies/Transparencies**

All blackline masters including assessment, transparency, and DPP masters are also on the Teacher Resource CD.

Student Books
Decimal Hex (*Discovery Assignment Book* Pages 179–181)

Assessment Tools
Observational Assessment Record (*Unit Resource Guide* Pages 13–14)

Name _____ Date _____

Decimal Hex

Players

This is a game for two or three players.

Materials

- *Decimal Hex* Game Board on the following page
- two same color centimeter cubes or other game markers for each player
- one clear plastic spinner or pencil and paper clip

Rules

The goal of this game is to move two cubes or other markers from matching hexagons to opposite matching hexagons that all have the same number.

1. Each player places both of his or her cubes on two matching hexagons with the same number. The target hexagons are the matching ones with the same number on the other side of the game board.

2. The first player spins the spinner.

3. If "Greater Than or Equal To" shows, the player can move one cube to a neighboring hexagon with a number that is greater than or equal to the number in the hexagon where the cube is now.

4. If "Less Than or Equal To" shows, the player can move one cube to a neighboring hexagon with a number that is less than or equal to the number in the hexagon where the cube is now.

5. The player does not have to move a cube during his or her turn.

6. More than one cube can be on the same hexagon at the same time.

7. Players take turns spinning the spinner and moving cubes.

8. The first player to get both cubes to his or her target hexagons is the winner.

Decimal Hex   DAB • Grade 4 • Unit 10 • Lesson 5 **179**

Discovery Assignment Book - page 179

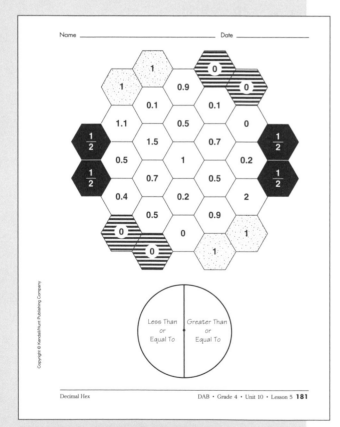

Discovery Assignment Book - page 181

Teaching the Activity

To begin, students read directions on the *Decimal Hex* Game Pages in the *Discovery Assignment Book*. Each player places two same-color centimeter cubes on two matching hexagons with the same number. The goal is to get the two cubes to the matching hexagons with the same number on the opposite side of the board. To move, a player spins the spinner. If the spinner shows greater than or equal to, the player can move to an adjacent hexagon with a number that is greater than or equal to his or her current position. If the spinner shows less than or equal to, the player moves to an adjacent hexagon with a number that is less than or equal to his or her current position. Students can model the decimals and fractions with base-ten pieces and use the pieces to make comparisons.

Homework and Practice

Encourage students to take home *Decimal Hex* to play with their families. Students will need their *Decimal Hex* Game Pages from the *Discovery Assignment Book*.

Assessment

Use the *Observational Assessment Record* to note students' abilities to compare and order decimals.

Estimated Class Sessions

1

At a Glance

Teaching the Activity

1. Students read the rules on the *Decimal Hex* Game Pages in the *Discovery Assignment Book*.
2. Students play *Decimal Hex*.

Homework

Students take home the *Decimal Hex* Game Pages. They play the game with family members.

Assessment

Use the *Observational Assessment Record* to note students' abilities to compare and order decimals.

Notes:

Alberto in TenthsLand

Lesson Overview

Estimated Class Sessions

1

Alberto falls asleep in the library and has a dream about a place called TenthsLand. He has a series of adventures in which he meets the Ten Percent Taxer, the Tenth-i-Pede, and the Centimeter Ruler. His dream ends when Mrs. Carroll, the librarian, gently shakes him awake.

Key Content

- Finding 10 percent of a number.
- Measuring to the nearest tenth of a centimeter.
- Multiplying by ten and by one-tenth.

Key Vocabulary

- 10%

Math Facts

DPP item W is a quiz on the division facts for the twos and threes. Task X asks students to solve a division problem, write a story about it, and draw a picture.

Homework

1. Have students read and discuss the *Adventure Book* with family members.
2. Assign Part 6 of the Home Practice.

Assessment

Use DPP Bit W to assess students on the division facts for the twos and threes.

Materials List

Supplies and Copies

Student	Teacher
Supplies for Each Student • calculator	**Supplies**
Copies	**Copies/Transparencies**

All blackline masters including assessment, transparency, and DPP masters are also on the Teacher Resource CD.

Student Books
TenthsLand (*Adventure Book* Pages 45–56)

Daily Practice and Problems and Home Practice
DPP items W–X (*Unit Resource Guide* Page 29)
Home Practice Part 6 (*Discovery Assignment Book* Page 158)

Note: Classrooms whose pacing differs significantly from the suggested pacing of the units should use the Math Facts Calendar in Section 4 of the *Facts Resource Guide* to ensure students receive the complete math facts program.

Daily Practice and Problems

Suggestions for using the DPPs are on page 115.

W. Bit: Quiz on 2s and 3s Division Facts
(URG p. 29)

A. $8 \div 2 =$	B. $30 \div 3 =$
C. $16 \div 2 =$	D. $9 \div 3 =$
E. $12 \div 2 =$	F. $21 \div 3 =$
G. $15 \div 3 =$	H. $4 \div 2 =$
I. $10 \div 2 =$	J. $27 \div 3 =$
K. $14 \div 2 =$	L. $12 \div 3 =$
M. $6 \div 3 =$	N. $24 \div 3 =$
O. $2 \div 1 =$	P. $18 \div 3 =$
Q. $18 \div 2 =$	R. $3 \div 3 =$
S. $20 \div 2 =$	

X. Task: Dividing It Up (URG p. 29)

$26 \div 8 = ?$ Write a story for $26 \div 8$.
Then draw a picture. Include any remainder in your picture.

TIMS Tip

You may want to read the story twice—once for the basic plot, and once again to draw out the mathematics.

Discussion Prompts

This story is based on *Alice in Wonderland,* especially her adventures when she follows the White Rabbit down the rabbit hole. Students familiar with Alice may enjoy this story more.

Page 46

*   *What experiment might Alberto be thinking of?*

Bouncing Ball

*   *How could he predict how high a basketball would bounce if it were dropped from 10 feet?*

Gather data for lesser heights, graph it, and extrapolate. Or drop it from 5 feet and double the bounce height.

*   *What could the white mouse be doing with a calculator?*

Alberto in TenthsLand

Alberto was reading a book in the library when it happened. The book was about basketball, Alberto's favorite game, but Alberto had played basketball all morning, and he was feeling sleepy and dull. He had begun to wonder how high a basketball would bounce if it were dropped from the rim, 10 feet up. He didn't know how he could find out since he couldn't reach that high to drop the ball. He thought the problem was like something he had done in school, but he couldn't remember exactly what.

Then he saw it. A small white mouse ran across the library floor and disappeared into a heating vent. Seeing a mouse was not unusual since the library was old. Alberto was not even especially surprised to see that this mouse was dressed in sweats and high-tops. But when the mouse pulled out a calculator and started pushing buttons furiously as he scurried along, Alberto jumped up and hurried after him.

46   AB • Grade 4 • Unit 10 • Lesson 6

Adventure Book - page 46

Page 47

- *What do you notice about the trees in TenthsLand? What about the sun?*

The trees are divided into ten parts. The sun has ten points.

- *Why does that make sense in a place called TenthsLand?*

Because tenths require dividing things into ten parts.

Adventure Book - page 47

Page 48

- *What do you think the Ten-X-Sizer might do?*
- *Why is Alberto saying good-bye to his feet?*

Because they are getting so far away.

Adventure Book - page 48

Alberto in TenthsLand

The view from high above the trees was lovely, but now Alberto was farther than ever from being able to get through the tiny door and into the wonderful garden. The disappointment was too much for poor Alberto, and he began to cry. He sat down and shed huge tears.

After a few minutes of crying, Alberto noticed another machine in the clearing, and he wondered why he hadn't noticed this one before either. This machine was very much like the first machine; only the words on the tower were different. On the new machine was written, "Tenth-X-Sizer."

AB · Grade 4 · Unit 10 · Lesson 6   **49**

Adventure Book - page 49

Page 49

- *How tall would you be if you were ten times as tall as you are now? As tall as the ceiling? As tall as the school building? A tree? A skyscraper?*

Fourth graders are normally between 50 and 60 inches. Since $10 \times 55 = 550$ inches or about 46 feet, this could be the height of a building.

- *How long would your foot be? Draw a picture of your ten-times-as-long footprint.*
- *How long would your pencil be?*
- *What do you think the Tenth-X-Sizer will do?*

Alberto in TenthsLand

Alberto thought that he might as well try this machine too, as he figured he could be no worse off than he was already. It was hard for him to fit on the machine, but as soon as he pushed the button he felt himself shrinking, shrinking, shrinking. In a moment, he was back to his proper size.

"If one push can do so much," thought Alberto, "I wonder what another will do." Alberto pushed the Tenth-X-Sizer button again and to his delight found himself shrinking once more. Luckily, he did not shrink away to nothing, but stopped at just the perfect height to fit through the tiny door in the tree. Immediately, Alberto went through the door and found himself in the beautiful garden.

50   AB · Grade 4 · Unit 10 · Lesson 6

Adventure Book - page 50

Page 50

- *How tall would you be if you were one-tenth as tall as you are now? Find an object in the classroom that is close to this height.*

Fourth graders are about 55 inches tall. One-tenth of 55 inches is 5.5 inches, so look for objects that are between 5 and 6 inches such as a calculator or a sharpened pencil.

- *How long would your foot be? How long would your pencil be?*
- *How many times could Alberto push the Tenth-X-Sizer button before he shrank to nothing?*

No matter how many times he pushed the button, he would never become nothing. He would get smaller and smaller, but there would always be a little bit left.

Page 51

- *Why does the Ten Percent Taxer have 1040 written on him?*

That's the number of the form for filing federal income tax returns in the United States.

- *What do you notice about the Ten Percent Taxer?*

He's divided into ten parts.

- *What do people really get for the taxes they pay?*

Schools, roads, national defense, help for poor people, foreign aid, food inspection, environmental protection, parks, police, and so on.

- *What is 10 percent of the things Alberto has?*

Discuss with students that 10% means 10 out of 100 or one-tenth. Students can find 10% of the items by using a calculator to divide by 10. Students who completed Unit 6 Lesson 5 can also move the decimal point one place to the left and round or truncate the answer.

He has 22 marbles, 39¢, 11 pieces of gum, and some string. Ten percent of these is roughly two marbles, 4¢, and one piece of gum. To find 10 percent of the string, the Ten Percent Taxer will have to fold it into ten equal parts or measure it.

- *What is 10 percent of 30 marbles? Of 70¢? Of 150 cm?*

3 marbles, 7¢, 15 cm. Repeat for other amounts.

Page 53

- *What animal does the Tenth-i-Pede's name remind you of?*

Centipede.

- *What do the word parts of centipede mean?*

Centi- is from the Latin for 100; *pede* is from the Latin word for foot. A centipede doesn't really have 100 feet, but it does have quite a few.

- *What other words can you think of that have cent- in them?*

Centimeter, cent, centigrade, century.

- *What do those words mean?*

$\frac{1}{100}$ of a meter, $\frac{1}{100}$ of a dollar, a temperature scale with 100 degrees between the freezing and boiling temperatures of water, a period of 100 years.

"Stop!" cried an odd creature who looked like a large piece of paper. "I am the Ten Percent Taxer. Pay your taxes at once or go to jail!"

"Taxes?" replied Alberto. "What are taxes?"

"Taxes buy civilization," answered the Ten Percent Taxer. "Now, show me what you have and I will take 10 percent. You must pay $\frac{1}{10}$ of what you have."

Alberto emptied his pockets. He had a bag of marbles, a quarter, a dime, four pennies, a half-empty package of chewing gum, and some kite string.

AB • Grade 4 • Unit 10 • Lesson 6   **51**

Adventure Book - page 51

Alberto gathered up his other things and looked around. He was startled to see what looked like a large caterpillar on the branch of a nearby tree. It seemed that the creature had been watching for some time.

"Who are you?" asked the creature.

"I'm not quite sure," answered Alberto. "I know who I was this morning when I got up, but I've changed several times since then, and now I'm not sure anymore. Who are you?"

"I'm the Tenth-i-Pede," replied the creature, who was beginning to disappear. The last three tenths were already gone and several more were fading fast. "If you don't know who you are, do you at least know what you're doing?"

Alberto answered, "I'm trying to find the white mouse. Have you seen him?"

"White mouse?" repeated the Tenth-i-Pede, who by this time was almost entirely gone. "White mouse? Look for the Centimeter Ruler. The white mouse works for her." And with that, the Tenth-i-Pede faded away the rest of the way, except for a faint outline of his smile, which lingered a minute or two longer.

AB • Grade 4 • Unit 10 • Lesson 6   **53**

Adventure Book - page 53

Alberto in TenthsLand

"Come here, stand next to me!" shouted the Centimeter Ruler. "Now, Mr. Mouse, how tall is he?"

"About 24 cm," answered the white mouse.

"You ninny! He's nowhere near 24 cm!" shouted the Centimeter Ruler.

"I meant to say that 10 percent of the string is about 24 cm," answered the mouse. "This fellow looks about 15.6 cm tall."

"Now, that's more like it!" shouted the Centimeter Ruler. "Now, you, Ten Percent Taxer, get his shirt and pants—we need 10 percent of those too."

At that, the Ten Percent Taxer and the Centimeter Ruler began to grab Alberto's shirt, trying to pull it off.

"No! No!" shouted Alberto. "That's my shirt. Leave me alone!"

The Centimeter Ruler, the Ten Percent Taxer, and the white mouse all tugged and pulled at Alberto's shirt. Alberto gave a shout of anger and tried to beat them off. Then he found himself sitting back in the library. Mrs. Carroll, the librarian, was gently shaking his shoulder. "Wake up! Alberto, wake up!" she said. "You've been asleep for a very long time. You must go now; we're closing."

AB • Grade 4 • Unit 10 • Lesson 6   **55**

Adventure Book - page 55

Alberto in TenthsLand

"Oh! What an amazing dream!" said Alberto as he gathered his books and hurried home to tell his mother about his strange dream.

Mrs. Carroll shook her head and smiled. Then, as she was closing up for the night, she saw a small white mouse scurry into an old heat vent. "How odd," she thought, "for a moment it looked as though that mouse was wearing sweats and high-tops."

56   AB • Grade 4 • Unit 10 • Lesson 6

Adventure Book - page 56

Page 55

• *What is 10 percent of 237 cm?*

About 24 cm. Exactly, 23.7 cm.

• *What is 10 percent of 250 cm? Of 500 cm?*

25 cm, 50 cm. Repeat for other lengths.

Page 56

• *Why is the librarian named Mrs. Carroll?*

Because the pseudonym or pen name of Charles Dodgson, author of *Alice in Wonderland,* was Lewis Carroll, and this story is based on some of Alice's adventures.

Math Facts

DPP Task X asks students to solve a division problem, write a story about it, and draw a picture.

Homework and Practice

- Read and discuss the *Adventure Book* with someone at home.
- Assign Part 6 of the Home Practice.

Answers for Part 6 of the Home Practice are in the Answer Key at the end of this lesson and at the end of this unit.

Assessment

DPP Bit W is a short quiz on the division facts for the twos and threes.

Literature Connection

- Carroll, Lewis. *The Annotated Alice: The Definitive Edition. Alice's Adventures in Wonderland;* and *Through the Looking-Glass and What Alice Found There.* Introduction by Martin Gardner. Illustrated by John Tenniel. W.W. Norton & Company, New York, 1999.

Name _____ Date _____

PART 6 Playing at the Park

1. A. When Shannon and her family arrived at the park on Saturday, Shannon counted 3 children on *each* of the following: the slide, the swings, the monkey bars, and the merry-go-round. How many children were at the park when Shannon arrived?

   B. If there were 8 more children than adults at the park, how many adults were at the park?

2. A used car dealer is across the street from the park. Shannon's dad looked at some cars while Shannon and her sister played at the park. He liked two different cars. One car costs $4550 and the other costs $3775. What is the difference in price of the two cars?

3. Shannon treated her little sister and her mother to a treat. At a nearby stand she bought two cans of juice at 65¢ each and three popsicles at 85¢ each. She gave the vendor $5.00. How much change will Shannon receive?

4. While playing in the park, Shannon's family saw a 5 kilometer race. 235 people were signed up to participate, but only 178 arrived the day of the race. How many people did not show up for the race?

5. A. Last summer, the park district raised money for new playground equipment. In June, $565 was raised. In July, $438 was raised. In August, $395 was raised. How much money was raised for new playground equipment?

   B. How much money do they need to raise in September to reach their goal of $1500?

158 DAB • Grade 4 • Unit 10   USING DECIMALS

Discovery Assignment Book - page 158 (Answers on p. 116)

<table>
<tr><td>

Name _____ Date _____

PART 6 Playing at the Park

I. A. When Shannon and her family arrived at the park on Saturday, Shannon counted 3 children on *each* of the following: the slide, the swings, the monkey bars, and the merry-go-round. How many children were at the park when Shannon arrived?

   B. If there were 8 more children than adults at the park, how many adults were at the park?

2. A used car dealer is across the street from the park. Shannon's dad looked at some cars while Shannon and her sister played at the park. He liked two different cars. One car costs $4550 and the other costs $3775. What is the difference in price of the two cars?

3. Shannon treated her little sister and her mother to a treat. At a nearby stand she bought two cans of juice at 65¢ each and three popsicles at 85¢ each. She gave the vendor $5.00. How much change will Shannon receive?

4. While playing in the park, Shannon's family saw a 5 kilometer race. 235 people were signed up to participate, but only 178 arrived the day of the race. How many people did not show up for the race?

5. A. Last summer, the park district raised money for new playground equipment. In June, $565 was raised. In July, $438 was raised. In August, $395 was raised. How much money was raised for new playground equipment?

   B. How much money do they need to raise in September to reach their goal of $1500?

158 DAB • Grade 4 • Unit 10   USING DECIMALS

</td></tr>
</table>

Discovery Assignment Book - page 158

Discovery Assignment Book (p. 158)

Home Practice*

Part 6. Playing at the Park

I. **A.** 12 children

   B. 4 adults

2. $775

3. $1.15

4. 57 people

5. **A.** $1398

   B. $102

*Answers for all the Home Practice in the *Discovery Assignment Book* are at the end of the unit.

Discovery Assignment Book (p. 155)

Part 2. Missing Numbers and Big Numbers

I. A. $n = 4$

   B. $n = 6$

   C. $n = 30$

   D. $n = 200$

   E. $n = 30$

   F. $n = 3$

2. A. 45,089; 45,676; 45,788; 47,998; 48,654; 54,673

   B. 49,000

   C. 45,100

3. Answers will vary. Possible answers are:

   A. $600,000 + 30,000 = 630,000$

   B. $2,700,000 + 4,000,000 = 6,700,000$

   C. $400,000 - 100,000 = 300,000$

Name _____ Date _____

Unit 10 Home Practice

PART 1 Triangle Flash Cards: 2s and 3s

Study for the quiz on the division facts for the 2s and 3s. Take home your *Triangle Flash Cards* and your list of facts you need to study.

Here's how to use the flash cards. Ask a family member to choose one flash card at a time. He or she should cover the corner containing either the square or the circle. This number will be the answer to a division fact. Solve a division problem with the two uncovered numbers.

Your teacher will tell you when the quiz on the 2s and 3s will be. Remember to concentrate on one small group of facts each night—about 8 to 10 facts. Also, remember to study only those facts you cannot answer correctly and quickly.

PART 2 Missing Numbers and Big Numbers

1. What number must n be to make each number sentence true? After you have decided on a number for n, check your work by multiplying.
   A. $n \times 20 = 80$ B. $300 \times n = 1800$ C. $90 \times n = 2700$

   D. $50 \times n = 10,000$ E. $n \times 50 = 1500$ F. $70 \times n = 210$

2. A. Write the following numbers in order from smallest to largest.
   45,676   54,673   45,788   48,654   47,998   45,089

   B. Round 48,654 to the nearest thousand.

   C. Round 45,089 to the nearest hundred.

3. Use convenient numbers to estimate the answers to the following problems. Record number sentences to show your thinking.
   A. $608,965 + 28,696$ B. $2,657,223 + 3,908,700$ C. $378,904 - 99,645$

USING DECIMALS   DAB • Grade 4 • Unit 10 **155**

Discovery Assignment Book - page 155

Discovery Assignment Book (p. 156)

Part 3. Decimals

I. A. 3.3

   B. 3.6

   C. 3.03

   D. 4.4
      3.03; 3.3; 3.6; 4.4

2. Answers will vary.

3. A. 1 dm, 23 cm, 0.45 m, 0.6 m, 55 dm

   B. 1.03 m, 1.24 m, 1.5 m, 1 m and 8 dm

Name _____ Date _____

PART 3 Decimals

1. Numbers are represented in base-ten shorthand below. The flat is one whole. Label each of the following with its correct number. Then put the numbers in order from least to greatest.

   A.

   B.

   C.

   D.

2. Write a decimal for each of the following. Then, show your decimal using base-ten shorthand. The flat is one whole. Find a number that is:
   A. Between 8 and 9   B. Between 4 and 4.5

   C. Just a little bigger than 8   D. Between $\frac{1}{2}$ and 2

3. For each of the two problems below, put the measurements in order from shortest to longest.
   A. 0.6 m   23 cm   1 dm   0.45 m   55 dm

   B. 1.5 m   1 m and 8 dm   1.03 meter   1.24 meter

156 DAB • Grade 4 • Unit 10   USING DECIMALS

Discovery Assignment Book - page 156

Name _____ Date _____

PART 4 School Supplies

Linda and her brother are buying school supplies. Notebooks are on sale for 39¢ each. Pencils are 4 for $1.00. A set of markers costs $2.98. Folders are 10 for $1.00.

1. Linda needs 3 notebooks, 1 set of markers, 1 folder, and 8 pencils. Estimate the cost of Linda's school supplies. Write number sentences to show your thinking.

2. Linda's brother needs 5 notebooks, 1 set of markers, 3 folders, and 4 pencils. Estimate the cost of his school supplies. Write number sentences to show your thinking.

3. What is the exact cost of each child's supplies? (There is no tax.)

4. What is the difference in price between the two children's supplies? Write a number sentence to show how you solved the problem.

PART 5 Addition, Subtraction, and Multiplication

Solve the following problems using paper and pencil or mental math. Estimate to make sure your answers are reasonable.

1. A. $68 - 49 =$ B. $167 + 67 =$ C. $284 + 238 =$ D. $432 - 197 =$

   E. $47 \times 9 =$ F. $26 \times 7 =$ G. $34 \times 9 =$ H. $23 \times 8 =$

2. Explain your estimation strategy for Question 1F.

3. Explain a possible mental math strategy for Question 1D.

USING DECIMALS   DAB • Grade 4 • Unit 10 **157**

Discovery Assignment Book - page 157

Discovery Assignment Book (p. 157)

Part 4. School Supplies

1. $3 \times \$0.40 = \$1.20$;
   $\$1.20 + \$3 + \$0.10 + \$2 = \$6.30$

2. $5 \times \$0.40 = \$2$;
   $\$2 + \$3 + \$0.30 + \$1 = \$6.30$

3. Linda: $6.25
   Linda's brother: $6.23

4. $\$6.25 - \$6.23 = \$0.02$ or 2¢

Part 5. Addition, Subtraction, and Multiplication

1. A. 19   B. 234
   C. 522   D. 235
   E. 423   F. 182
   G. 306   H. 184

2. Possible strategy: 26×7 is close to 25×7. Skip count by 25s seven times: 25, 50, 75, 100, 125, 150, 175. 26×7 is about 175.

3. Possible strategy: $432 - 197$ is the same as $435 - 200 = 235$.

Name _____ Date _____

PART 6 Playing at the Park

1. A. When Shannon and her family arrived at the park on Saturday, Shannon counted 3 children on *each* of the following: the slide, the swings, the monkey bars, and the merry-go-round. How many children were at the park when Shannon arrived?

   B. If there were 8 more children than adults at the park, how many adults were at the park?

2. A used car dealer is across the street from the park. Shannon's dad looked at some cars while Shannon and her sister played at the park. He liked two different cars. One car costs $4550 and the other costs $3775. What is the difference in price of the two cars?

3. Shannon treated her little sister and her mother to a treat. At a nearby stand she bought two cans of juice at 65¢ each and three popsicles at 85¢ each. She gave the vendor $5.00. How much change will Shannon receive?

4. While playing in the park, Shannon's family saw a 5 kilometer race. 235 people were signed up to participate, but only 178 arrived the day of the race. How many people did not show up for the race?

5. A. Last summer, the park district raised money for new playground equipment. In June, $565 was raised. In July, $438 was raised. In August, $395 was raised. How much money was raised for new playground equipment?

   B. How much money do they need to raise in September to reach their goal of $1500?

158 DAB • Grade 4 • Unit 10   USING DECIMALS

Discovery Assignment Book - page 158

Discovery Assignment Book (p. 158)

Part 6. Playing at the Park

1. A. 12 children
   B. 4 adults

2. $775

3. $1.15

4. 57 people

5. A. $1398
   B. $102

Glossary

This glossary provides definitions of key vocabulary terms in the Grade 4 lessons. Locations of key vocabulary terms in the curriculum are included with each definition. Components Key: URG = *Unit Resource Guide* and SG = *Student Guide*.

A

Acre (URG Unit 6; SG Unit 6)
A measure of land area equal to 43,560 square feet.

Acute Angle (URG Unit 2 & Unit 9; SG Unit 2)
An angle that measures less than 90°.

All-Partials Algorithm
(URG Unit 7; SG Unit 7)
A paper-and-pencil method for solving multiplication problems. Each partial product is recorded on a separate line. (*See also* partial product.)

$$\begin{array}{r} 186 \\ \times\ 3 \\ \hline 18 \\ 240 \\ 300 \\ \hline 558 \end{array}$$

Angle (URG Unit 2; SG Unit 2)
The amount of turning or the amount of opening between two rays that have the same endpoint.

Angle of Turning (URG Unit 9)
The smallest angle through which a figure can be turned about the center of turning so that the figure coincides with itself.

Area (SG Unit 2)
The area of a shape is the amount of space it covers, measured in square units.

Array (URG Unit 4)
An array is an arrangement of elements into a rectangular pattern of (horizontal) rows and (vertical) columns.

Average (URG Unit 1 & Unit 5; SG Unit 1 & Unit 5)
A number that can be used to represent a typical value in a set of data. (*See also* mean and median.)

B

Base (of an exponent) (SG Unit 4)
When exponents are used, the number being multiplied. In $3^4 = 3 \times 3 \times 3 \times 3 = 81$, the 3 is the base and the 4 is the exponent. The 3 is multiplied by itself 4 times.

Base-Ten Board (URG Unit 3; SG Unit 3)
A tool to help children organize base-ten pieces when they are representing numbers.

Base-Ten Pieces (URG Unit 3; SG Unit 3)
A set of manipulatives used to model our number system as shown in the figure below. Note that a skinny is made of 10 bits, a flat is made of 100 bits, and a pack is made of 1000 bits.

Nickname	Picture	Shorthand
bit		
skinny		
flat		
pack		

Base-Ten Shorthand (URG Unit 3; SG Unit 3)
A pictorial representation of the base-ten pieces is shown in Unit 3.

Benchmarks (URG Unit 6; SG Unit 6)
Numbers convenient for comparing and ordering numbers, e.g., 0, $\frac{1}{2}$, 1 are convenient benchmarks for comparing and ordering fractions.

Best-Fit Line (URG Unit 5; SG Unit 5)
The line that comes closest to the points on a point graph.

Binning Data (URG Unit 13)
Placing data from a data set with a large number of values or large range into intervals in order to more easily see patterns in the data.

Bit (URG Unit 3 & Unit 6; SG Unit 3)
A cube that measures 1 cm on each edge. It is the smallest of the base-ten pieces and is often used to represent 1. (*See also* base-ten pieces.)

C

Categorical Variable (URG Unit 1; SG Unit 1)
Variables with values that are not numbers. (*See also* variable and value.)

Center of Turning (URG Unit 9; SG Unit 9)
A point on a plane figure around which it is turned. In particular, the point about which an object with turn symmetry is rotated.

Centimeter (SG Unit 10)
A unit of length in the metric system. A centimeter is $\frac{1}{100}$ of a meter.

Certain Event (URG Unit 14; SG Unit 14)
An event that has a probability of 1 (100%).

Common Fraction (URG Unit 10)
Any fraction that is written with a numerator and denominator that are whole numbers. For example, $\frac{3}{4}$ and $\frac{9}{4}$ are both common fractions. (*See also* decimal fraction.)

Commutative Property of Multiplication
(URG Unit 3 & Unit 4)
This is also known as the Order Property of Multiplication. Changing the order of the factors does not change the product. For example, $3 \times 5 = 5 \times 3 = 15$. Using variables, $n \times m = m \times n$.

Composite Number (URG Unit 4)
A number that has more than two distinct factors. For example, 9 has three factors (1, 3, 9) so it is a composite number.

Convenient Number (URG Unit 1 & Unit 7; SG Unit 7)
A number used in computation that is close enough to give a good estimate, but is also easy to compute with mentally, e.g., 25 and 30 are convenient numbers for 27.

Cubic Centimeter (URG Unit 8; SG Unit 8)
The volume of a cube that is one centimeter long on each edge.

D

Decimal (URG Unit 3)
1. A number written using the base-ten place value system.
2. A number containing a decimal point. (*See also* decimal fraction.)

Decimal Fraction (URG Unit 10)
A fraction written as a decimal. For example, 0.75 and 0.4 are decimal fractions and $\frac{75}{100}$ and $\frac{4}{10}$ are called common fractions.

Decimeter (URG Unit 10; SG Unit 10)
A unit of length in the metric system. A decimeter is $\frac{1}{10}$ of a meter.

Degree (URG Unit 2; SG Unit 2)
A degree (°) is a unit of measure for angles. There are 360 degrees in a circle.

Denominator (URG Unit 10 & Unit 12; SG Unit 10 & Unit 12)
The number below the line in a fraction. The denominator indicates the number of equal parts in which the unit whole is divided. For example, the 5 is the denominator in the fraction $\frac{2}{5}$. In this case the unit whole is divided into five equal parts.

Dividend (URG Unit 3; SG Unit 3)
The number that is divided in a division problem, e.g., 12 is the dividend in $12 \div 3 = 4$.

Divisible (URG Unit 7; SG Unit 7)
A number a is divisible by a number b, if there is no remainder when a is divided by b. For example, 12 is divisible by 4 ($12 \div 4 = 3$), but **not** by 5 ($12 \div 5 = 2$ R2).

Division Sentence (SG Unit 3)
A number sentence involving division.

Divisor (URG Unit 3 & Unit 8; SG Unit 3 & Unit 8)
In a division problem, the number by which another number is divided. In the problem $12 \div 4 = 3$, the 4 is the divisor, the 12 is the dividend, and the 3 is the quotient.

E

Edge (URG Unit 9; SG Unit 9)
A line segment where two faces of a three-dimensional figure meet.

Equilateral Triangle (URG Unit 2 & Unit 9; SG Unit 9)
A triangle with all sides and all angles equal.

Equivalent Fractions (URG Unit 12; SG Unit 12)
Fractions that have the same value, e.g., $\frac{2}{4} = \frac{1}{2}$.

Estimate (URG Unit 3, Unit 6, & Unit 7; SG Unit 7)
1. (verb) To find *about* how many.
2. (noun) An approximate number.

Even Number (SG Unit 4)
Numbers that are multiples of 2 (2, 4, 6, 8, etc.) are
called even numbers.

Exponent (URG Unit 4; SG Unit 4)
The number of times the base is multiplied by itself. In
$3^4 = 3 \times 3 \times 3 \times 3 = 81$, the 3 is the base and the 4 is
the exponent. The 3 is multiplied by itself 4 times.

Extrapolation (URG Unit 5; SG Unit 5)
Using patterns in data to make predictions or to estimate
values that lie beyond the range of values in the set of data.

F

Face (URG Unit 9; SG Unit 9)
A plane figure that is one side of a three-dimensional
figure.

Fact Family (URG Unit 3 & Unit 8; SG Unit 3 & Unit 8)
Related math facts, e.g., $3 \times 4 = 12$, $4 \times 3 = 12$,
$12 \div 3 = 4$, $12 \div 4 = 3$.

Factor (URG Unit 3 & Unit 4; SG Unit 3, Unit 4, &
   Unit 7)
1. In a multiplication problem, the numbers that are multiplied together. In the problem $3 \times 4 = 12$, 3 and 4
   are the factors.
2. Whole numbers that can be multiplied together to get
   a number. That is, numbers that divide a number
   evenly, e.g., 1, 2, 3, 4, 6, and 12 are all the factors
   of 12.

Factor Tree (URG Unit 4;
   SG Unit 4)
A diagram that shows the
prime factorization of a
number.

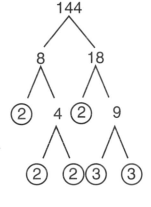

**Fair Game or Fair Number
   Cube** (URG Unit 14)
A game in which it is equally
likely that any player will win.
A number cube is fair if all
the faces are equally likely
to appear.

Fewest Pieces Rule (URG Unit 3 & Unit 10; SG Unit 3)
Using the least number of base-ten pieces to represent a
number. (*See also* base-ten pieces.)

Fixed Variables (URG Unit 1, Unit 2, & Unit 5;
   SG Unit 5)
Variables in an experiment that are held constant or not
changed.

Flat (URG Unit 3 & Unit 6; SG Unit 3)
A block that measures 1 cm $\times$ 10 cm $\times$ 10 cm.
It is one of the base-ten pieces
and is often used to represent
100. (*See also* base-ten pieces.)

Forgiving Method of Division
   (URG Unit 13; SG Unit 13)
A paper-and-pencil method for division
in which successive partial quotients
are chosen and partial products are
subtracted from the dividend, until
the remainder is less than the divisor.
The sum of the partial quotients is the
quotient. For example, $644 \div 7$ can be
solved as shown at the right. This
method of division is called the forgiving method because it "forgives" estimates of the
partial quotients that are too low.

```
              92
        7 | 644
            140  | 20
            504
            350  | 50
            154
            140  | 20
             14
             14  |  2
              0  | 92
```

Front-End Estimation (URG Unit 3)
Estimation by looking at the left-most digit.

Function (URG Unit 15)
A rule that assigns to any input number exactly one out-
put number. More generally, a rule that assigns to the elements of one set (the domain) exactly one element of
another set (the target).

G

H

Hexagon (URG Unit 2)
A six-sided polygon.

Hieroglyphics (URG Unit 11)
An ancient Egyptian form of writing.

I

Identity Property of Multiplication (URG Unit 3)
This is also known as the Property of One for
Multiplication. One times any number is that number.
Using variables, $n \times 1 = n$.

Impossible Event (URG Unit 14; SG Unit 14)
An event that has a probability of 0 or 0%.

Infinite (URG Unit 9)
Cannot be counted in a finite amount of time. More than
any number.

Interpolation (URG Unit 5; SG Unit 5)
Making predictions or estimating values that lie between
data points in a set of data.

Intersect (SG Unit 9)
To meet or cross.

J

K

L

Likely Event (URG Unit 14; SG Unit 14)
An event that has a high probability of occurring.

Line (URG Unit 9; SG Unit 9)
A set of points that form a straight path extending infinitely in two directions.

Line Segment (URG Unit 9; SG Unit 9)
A part of a line between and including two points called the endpoints.

Line of Symmetry (URG Unit 9; SG Unit 9)
A line is a line of symmetry for a plane figure if, when the figure is folded along this line, the two parts match exactly.

Line Symmetry (URG Unit 9; SG Unit 9)
A figure has line symmetry if it has at least one line of symmetry.

Liter (SG Unit 8)
Metric unit used to measure volume. A liter is a little more than a quart.

M

Manipulated Variable (URG Unit 5 & Unit 10; SG Unit 5)
In an experiment, the variable with values known at the beginning of the experiment. The experimenter often chooses these values before data is collected. The manipulated variable is often called the independent variable.

Mass (URG Unit 8 & Unit 15; SG Unit 15)
The amount of matter in an object.

Mean (URG Unit 1 & Unit 5; SG Unit 5)
An average of a set of numbers that is found by adding the values of the data and dividing by the number of values.

Measurement Division (URG Unit 4)
Division as equal grouping. The total number of objects and the number of objects in each group are known. The number of groups is the unknown. For example, tulip bulbs come in packages of 8. If 216 bulbs are sold, how many packages are sold?

Measurement Error
The unavoidable error that occurs due to the limitations inherent to any measurement instrument.

Median (URG Unit 1 & Unit 5; SG Unit 1 & Unit 5)
For a set with an odd number of data arranged in order, it is the middle number. For an even number of data arranged in order, it is the number halfway between the two middle numbers.

Megabit (URG Unit 6)
A base-ten model that is a cube with an edge of length 100 cm. It represents 1,000,000 since it has a volume of 1,000,000 cubic cm.

Meniscus (URG Unit 8; SG Unit 8)
The curved surface formed when a liquid creeps up the side of a container (for example, a graduated cylinder).

Meter (SG Unit 10)
A unit of length in the metric system. A meter is a bit more that 39 inches.

Milliliter (ml) (URG Unit 8; SG Unit 8)
A measure of capacity in the metric system that is the volume of a cube that is one centimeter long on each side.

Millimeter (SG Unit 10)
A unit of length in the metric system. A millimeter is one-thousandth of a meter, i.e., one-tenth of a centimeter.

Millions Period (URG Unit 6; SG Unit 6)
The sequence of digits (if any) in the millions place, the ten-millions place, and the hundred millions place. In the number 12,**456**,789,987 the millions period is in bold type.

Multiple (URG Unit 4 & Unit 7; SG Unit 4 & Unit 7)
A number is a multiple of another number if it is evenly divisible by that number. For example, 12 is a multiple of 2 since 2 divides 12 evenly.

Multiplicand (URG Unit 11)
Either of the numbers being multiplied in a multiplication problem.

N

Negative Number (URG Unit 3; SG Unit 3)
A number less than zero; a number to the left of zero on a horizontal number line.

Net (URG Unit 9; SG Unit 9)
A way of representing the surface of a three-dimensional solid in two-dimensions. A net can be obtained by cutting the surface along edges until it can be laid flat on a plane.

Number Sentence
An equation or inequality with numbers. For example, $3 \times 2 + 5 = 10 + 1$ and $2 < 3 + 1$

Numeral (URG Unit 3)
A symbol used to represent a number.

Numerator (URG Unit 10 & Unit 12; SG Unit 10 & Unit 12)
The number written above the line in a fraction. For example, the 2 is the numerator in the fraction $\frac{2}{5}$. (*See also* denominator.)

Numerical Variable (URG Unit 1; SG Unit 1)
Variables with values that are numbers. (*See also* variable and value.)

O

Obtuse Angle (URG Unit 2 & Unit 9; SG Unit 2)
An angle that measures more than 90°.

Odd Number (SG Unit 4)
Numbers that are not multiples of 2 (1, 3, 5 ,7, etc.) are called odd numbers.

Ones Period (URG Unit 6; SG Unit 6)
The sequence of digits (if any) in the ones place, the tens place, and the hundreds place. In the number 12,456,789,**987** the ones period is in bold type.

Operation (SG Unit 7)
A process that takes two numbers and results in a third. This, more precisely, is called a binary operation. For example, addition, subtraction, multiplication, and division are operations.

Order of Operations (URG Unit 7; SG Unit 7)
A convention that determines how to find the value of an expression that has more than one operation.

P

Pack (URG Unit 3; SG Unit 3)
A cube that measures 10 cm on each edge. It is one of the base-ten pieces and is often used to represent 1000. (*See also* base-ten pieces.)

Papyrus (URG Unit 11)
A type of writing paper used by the ancient Egyptians.

Parallel Lines (URG Unit 9; SG Unit 9)
Lines that are in the same direction. In the plane, parallel lines are lines that do not intersect.

Parallelogram (URG Unit 9; SG Unit 9)
A quadrilateral with two pairs of parallel sides.

Partitive Division (URG Unit 4 & Unit 13)
Division as equal sharing. The total number of objects and the number of groups are known. The number of objects in each group is the unknown. For example, Frank has 144 marbles that he divides equally into 6 groups. How many marbles are in each group?

Perimeter (URG Unit 2; SG Unit 2)
The distance around a two-dimensional shape.

Period (URG Unit 6; SG Unit 6)
A group of three places in a large number, starting on the right, often separated by commas as shown at the right.

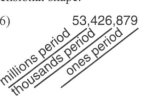

Perpendicular (URG Unit 9; SG Unit 9)
Perpendicular lines are lines that meet at right angles.

Perspective (URG Unit 9)
The art of drawing solid objects on a flat surface so that it produces the same impression as do the actual objects when viewed from a particular point.

Point (URG Unit 9)
An exact position in the plane or in space.

Polygon (URG Unit 9; SG Unit 9)
A two-dimensional connected figure made of line segments in which each endpoint of every side meets with an endpoint of exactly one other side.

Polyhedron (URG Unit 9)
A connected geometric solid whose surface is made of polygons.

Portfolio (URG Unit 2)
A collection of student work that shows how a student's skills, attitudes, and knowledge change over time.

Positive Number (URG Unit 3; SG Unit 3)
A number greater than zero; a number to the right of zero on a horizontal number line.

Powers of Two (URG Unit 6; SG Unit 6)
2 multiplied by itself a certain number of times. $2^1 = 2$, $2^2 = 2 \times 2 = 4$, $2^3 = 2 \times 2 \times 2 = 8$, etc.

Prime Factor (URG Unit 4; SG Unit 4)
A factor of a number that is itself prime.

Prime Number (URG Unit 4; SG Unit 4)
A number that has exactly two factors, itself and 1. For example, 7 has exactly two distinct factors, 1 and 7.

Prism (URG Unit 9; SG Unit 9)
A polyhedron that has two congruent faces, called bases, that are parallel to each other, and all other faces are parallelograms. If the other faces are rectangles the prism is called a right prism.

Prisms   Not a prism

Probability (URG Unit 14; SG Unit 14)
A number from 0 to 1 (0% to 100%) that describes how likely an event is to happen. The closer that the probability of an event is to one, the more likely the event will happen.

Product (URG Unit 3; SG Unit 3 & Unit 4)
The answer to a multiplication problem. In the problem $3 \times 4 = 12$, 12 is the product.

Q

Quadrilateral (URG Unit 9; SG Unit 2 & Unit 9)
A polygon with four sides. (*See also* polygon.)

Quick Paper-and-Pencil Method for Addition
   (URG Unit 3; SG Unit 3)
A traditional method for
adding multidigit numbers.
See example at right:

$$\begin{array}{r} \overset{1\ 1}{1326} \\ +575 \\ \hline 1901 \end{array}$$

Quick Paper-and-Pencil Method for Subtraction (SG Unit 3)
A traditional method for subtraction.
For example:

$$\begin{array}{r} 1237 \\ -459 \\ \hline 778 \end{array}$$

Quotient (URG Unit 3 & Unit 13; SG Unit 3 & Unit 8)
The answer to a division problem. In the problem $12 \div 3 = 4$, the 4 is the quotient.

R

Ray (URG Unit 9; SG Unit 9)
A part of a line that has one endpoint and extends indefinitely in one direction.

Recording Sheet (URG Unit 3; SG Unit 3)
A place value chart used for addition and subtraction problems.

Rectangle (URG Unit 2 & Unit 9)
A quadrilateral with four right angles.

Reflex Angle (URG Unit 2)
An angle larger than 180° but less than 360°.

Regular (URG Unit 9)
A polygon is regular if all sides are of equal length and all angles are equal.

Remainder (URG Unit 13)
Something that remains or is left after a whole number division problem. The portion of the dividend that is not evenly divisible by the divisor, e.g., $16 \div 5 = 3$ with 1 as a remainder.

Responding Variable (URG Unit 5 & Unit 10; SG Unit 5)
The variable whose values result from the experiment. Experimenters find the values of the responding variable by doing the experiment. The responding variable is often called the dependent variable.

Rhombus (URG Unit 2)
A quadrilateral with four sides of equal length.

Right Angle (URG Unit 2 & Unit 9; SG Unit 2)
An angle that measures 90°.

Roman Numeral (URG Unit 3; SG Unit 3)
A system of representing numbers used by the Romans. The symbol I represents 1, V represents five, X represents ten, etc.

Rounded Number (URG Unit 6 & Unit 7)
See rounding.

Rounding (URG Unit 6)
Replacing a number with the nearest convenient number. Numbers are often rounded to the nearest whole number, ten, hundred, fifty, etc.

S

Skinny (URG Unit 3 & Unit 6; SG Unit 3)
A block that measures 1 cm × 1 cm
× 10 cm. It is one of the base-ten
pieces that is often used to represent 10.
(*See also* base-ten pieces.)

Solid (URG Unit 9; SG Unit 9)
A three-dimensional figure that has volume greater than 0.

Square (URG Unit 2)
A polygon with four equal sides and four right angles.

Square Inch (SG Unit 2)
The area of a square with a side length of one inch.

Square Number (URG Unit 4; SG Unit 4)
A number that is the result of multiplying a whole number by itself. For example, 36 is a square number since $36 = 6 \times 6$.

Square Root (URG Unit 15)
The square root of a number N is the number whose square is N. The symbol for square root is $\sqrt{\ }$. For example, the square root of 25 is 5, since $5 \times 5 = 25$. In symbols we write $\sqrt{25} = 5$. The square root of 26 is not a whole number.

Subtractive Principle (URG Unit 3; SG Unit 3)
A method of interpreting certain Roman numerals. For example, IX represents 9 while XI represents 11.

Super Bit (URG Unit 6)
A base-ten model that is a cube with an edge of length 10 cm. It represents 1,000 since it has a volume of 1,000 cubic centimeters. It is usually called a pack.

Super Flat (URG Unit 6)
A base-ten model that is a rectangular solid that measures 10 cm × 100 cm × 100 cm. It represents 100,000 since it has a volume of 100,000 cubic cm.

Super Skinny (URG Unit 6)
A base-ten model that is a rectangular solid that measures 10 cm × 10 cm × 100 cm. It represents 10,000 since it has a volume of 10,000 cubic cm.

Survey (SG Unit 13)
An investigation conducted by collecting data from a sample of a population and then analyzing it. Usually surveys are used to make predictions about the entire population.

T

Tally
A way of recording a count by making marks. Usually tallies are grouped in fives.

Ten Percent (10%) (URG Unit 6 & Unit 7)
10 out of every hundred or $\frac{1}{10}$.

Thousands Period (URG Unit 6; SG Unit 6)
The sequence of digits (if any) in the thousands place, the ten-thousands place, and the hundred-thousands place. In the number 12,456,**789**,987 the thousands period is in bold type.

TIMS Laboratory Method (URG Unit 1; SG Unit 1)
A method that students use to organize experiments and investigations. It involves four phases: draw, collect, graph, and explore. It is a way to help students learn about the scientific method.

Translational Symmetry (URG Unit 9)
A pattern has translational symmetry if there is a translation that moves the pattern so it coincides with itself.

Trapezoid (URG Unit 2)
A quadrilateral with exactly one pair of parallel sides.

Triangle (URG Unit 2)
A polygon with three sides.

Turn-Around Facts (URG Unit 3; SG Unit 3)
Multiplication facts that have the same factors but in a different order, e.g., $3 \times 4 = 12$ and $4 \times 3 = 12$. (*See also* commutative property of multiplication.)

Turn-Around Rule (URG Unit 4)
A term used to describe the commutative property of multiplication. (*See also* commutative property of multiplication.)

Turn Symmetry (URG Unit 9; SG Unit 9)
A figure has turn symmetry if it can be rotated around a point (called the center of turning) through an angle less than 360° and so that the turned figure matches the original.

Type of Turn Symmetry (URG Unit 9)
The number of times a figure coincides with itself when it is rotated about its center of turning. For example, a square has 4-fold turn symmetry. This is also called $\frac{1}{4}$ turn symmetry.

U

Undefined (Division by Zero) (URG Unit 13; SG Unit 13)
We say division by 0 is undefined because there is no number that satisfies the definition of division when 0 is the divisor. For example, if there were a number $N = 3 \div 0$, it would be the unique number N that makes $N \times 0 = 3$ a true statement. There is no such N.

Unlikely Event (URG Unit 14; SG Unit 14)
An event that has small probability.

V

Value (URG Unit 1; SG Unit 1)
The possible outcomes of a variable. For example, red, green, and blue are possible values for the variable *color*. Two meters and 1.65 meters are possible values for the variable *length*.

Variable (URG Unit 1; SG Unit 1)
1. An attribute or quantity that changes or varies. (*See also* categorical variable and numerical variable.)
2. A symbol that can stand for a variable.

Vertex (URG Unit 2 & Unit 9; SG Unit 2 & Unit 9)
The common endpoint of two rays or line segments.

Volume (URG Unit 8 & Unit 9; SG Unit 8)
The measure of the amount of space occupied by an object.

Volume by Displacement (SG Unit 8)
A way of measuring volume by measuring the amount of water (or some other fluid) it displaces.

W

Weight (URG Unit 15; SG Unit 15)
A measure of the pull of gravity on an object. One unit for measuring weight is the pound.

X

Y

Z

Zero Property of Multiplication (URG Unit 3)
Any number times zero is zero. Using variables, $n \times 0 = 0$.